Decline without Fall:
Romania under Ceausescu

by
Mark Almond

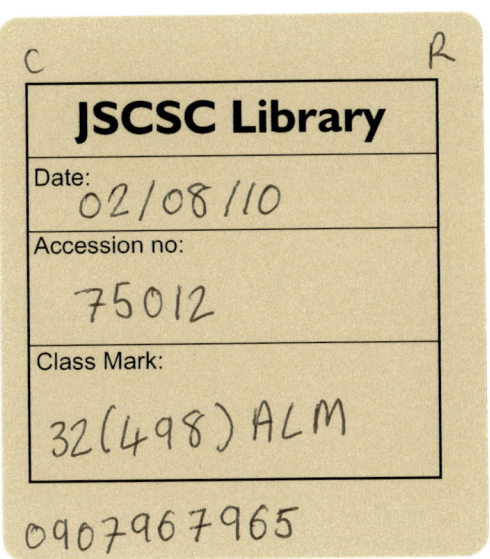
Alliance Publishers Ltd., for the
INSTITUTE FOR EU[ROPEAN DEFENCE AND STRAT]EGIC STUDIES

First published 1988
© INSTITUTE FOR EUROPEAN DEFENCE & STRATEGIC STUDIES

ISBN 0 907967 96 5

Designed by Reginald Cline MCSD MSTD
Typeset by TJB Photosetting Ltd, South Witham, Lincolnshire.
Printed by SR Press Ltd, Exeter

Contents

Preface

With the possible exception of the quasi-feudal backwater of Albania, the Romanians are easily the poorest and most oppressed nation in Europe. Unlike Albania, however, Romania has not always been sunk in a condition of static and hopeless immiseration. Nor have its people been accustomed to living in a state of bleak economic and cultural isolation, as they now do. By contemporary standards, pre-War Romania was far from impoverished, and its cities, especially its capital, were both culturally and economically vibrant.

Romania's present deprivations, highlighted by a near-total disregard for human rights, and by a uniformity of existence drab beyond compare, are the consequence of Marxist economic and social planning, to which the government of Nicolae Ceausescu has shown considerable fidelity. Beset with shortages, dislocations in supply and a top-heavy bureaucracy, the Romanian economy provides a classic illustration of the chaos which characterises the command system of allocating resources. Romania's political structure, meanwhile, remains in rigid conformity with Marxist notions of centralism. There is, as yet, little sign that its great human and economic costs, and the murmurings of industrial discontent which occurred in 1987, have brought the Romanian leadership to consider pragmatic answers to Romania's problems.

As the author of this European Security Study, Mark Almond, points out, Romania itself underwent a period of Gorbachev-style *perestroika* in the late 1960s and early 1970s, which included some measure of press and intellectual freedom. But its ultimate purpose was to concentrate power as never before in the hands of the ruling elite – in the form, as the much-repeated gibe puts it, of "socialism in one family". Its secondary effect was to convince many Western observers that Ceausescu was in fact following a secret liberal agenda.

Despite the extent of the country's economic deprivations and the severity of his restrictions, Ceausescu has not lacked friends in the West. Thanks to an outward show of independence in foreign policy, Romania has until recently enjoyed "most favoured nation" status in its trade with the United States, as well as generous support from the International Monetary Fund, while Ceausescu himself has received an extraordinary range of honours from Western institutions and heads of state.

Western enthusiasm for the Romanian dictator has at last cooled; but as Mr Almond suggests, it is an indictment of Western opinion that it has been the fate of Romania's architectural heritage, rather than that of its people, that has brought about the change. The lesson would seem to be a simple one: unless the victims of totalitarian rule include well-known intellectuals, with established reputations in the West, public opinion is unlikely to be moved, however brutally they may be treated. Moreover, so selective and patchy are the moral sensibilities of many Church leaders that not even the bulldozing of churches and monasteries has produced so much as an audible whisper of protest among Western churchmen.

Given that Ceausescu was lionised in the West because of the advice and pressure from Western Foreign Ministries, it is not altogether surprising that Foreign Ministers should not now be urging that the honours bestowed upon him be rescinded. What is remarkable, however, is that there has not been any pressure from any quarter for this to happen. Such a course of action would not merely be an empty gesture: Western support for Ceausescu has helped to legitimise and sustain a regime with one of the worst human rights records in the world, without achieving any lasting and tangible benefits for the West. Quite apart from its symbolic value, the withdrawal of the honours which enhance this facade of legitimacy would provide moral support for those seeking change from within.

The Institute is obliged to dissociate itself from the findings of its authors. But we are indebted to Mark Almond for his eloquent analysis of Romania's present political conditions and external relations, and for making forceful suggestions about how the West might use its moral and economic resources to bring about reform.

October 1988

GF

I. Introduction

"I care for the Romanians as I do for my glass when it is empty" – Bismarck

It is a striking testimony to the concern of Western opinion-makers for human rights and the fate of ordinary people that it was only when the President of Romania, Nicolae Ceausescu, began to demolish much of the historic centre of Bucharest that any attention was given to developments inside the country by the British press. Even then, the demolition of at least 24 churches and monasteries in the capital alone often excited more sympathy than the tragic fate of his human victims.

Until very recently, the internal policies of the communist regime in Romania were hardly ever mentioned, except as a bizarre and faintly comic throw-back to the Stalinist past, vividly contrasting with the sweetness and light emanating from Moscow. Stories of Ceausescu's nepotism, and of the grotesque cult surrounding his personality – and, more recently, that of his wife, Elena – made the joke about "socialism in one family" almost obligatory in the few reports on the country which appeared, usually filed from abroad. Even this negative publicity did little more than place the couple on a par with Ferdinand and Isabella Marcos of the Philippines.

Whatever bad news emerged of his internal policies was easily outweighed by the plaudits which Ceausescu regularly received for his foreign policy from Western heads of state and government. He was a "maverick", another Tito, trying to distance himself from the Soviet Union. He had "proved his independence" by participating in the 1984 Los Angeles Olympics, despite the Soviet boycott. A mixture of skilful disinformation, wishful thinking and gullibility ensured that the West accepted Ceausescu's own version of himself – as the "nationalist" communist ruler of a plucky country, successfully defending its independence with guile and courage against its giant Soviet neighbour. Just 10 years ago, at the peak of his popularity with the NATO states, Ceausescu was able to flit from the White House to Buckingham Palace like an old friend. He received honours denied even to Tito. In June 1978, he was rewarded for his apparent defiance of the Soviet Union by being the first communist head of state to be invited to stay in Buckingham Palace, where he had the pleasure of listening as the Queen herself assured him (in words dictated by Dr David Owen's Foreign and Commonwealth Office) that "today, we in Britain are impressed by the resolute stand which you have taken to sustain that independence."[1] At least she was not obliged to go as far as the Anglican Bishop of Southwark, whose dithyramb of praise – "each year I have noticed a higher standard of living" – for this "brave man", compared civil liberties in Britain to those in Romania. "There are different brands of dictatorship", the bishop enthused, praising the "exceedingly generous" treatment of the churches in Romania, a treatment of which "we in Britain might well be envious!"[2]

The debt crisis of the Warsaw Pact states attracted a little more attention to Romania in the early 1980s; but it was only the outbreak of serious rioting in Brasov, on 15 November 1987, which attracted real media interest in the West. Even then, the positive image of Ceausescu's regime lingered on. Nick Worrall, a reporter with the British Broadcasting Corporation, admitted that some people saw him as a *"virtual* dictator"; and when told that bread was rationed in Romania, he anxiously asked a studio expert: "Does he suffer from bad economic advice?" Perhaps Worrall's naive question should not be judged too harshly: even as late as May 1985, Helmut Sonnenfeldt, the former US National Security Adviser, was dismissing critics of Ceausescu's economic policies as being "influenced by Hungarian propaganda".[3]

The growing evidence of desperate popular discontent with the regime has coincided with the appearance of two volumes of memoirs, casting fresh light on the background to Ceausescu's extraordinarily successful cultivation of relations with the West. Both were written in a style, and with a passion, which would have led to their immediate dismissal by serious scholars and "sophisticated" observers everywhere, had not the clear evidence of developments in Romania made them credible. One of them, Ion Mihai Pacepa's *Red Horizons*, is presented in an unfortunate form by its publishers, as the flashback diary of Ceausescu's chief intelligence and security aide, covering his last weeks with "the Comrade" before his defection to the United States in 1978. Pacepa tells a depressing tale of double-dealing, and of the routine deception of the West, which formed part of a long-term plan to acquire Western intelligence, technical support and economic aid, and to influence Western diplomacy to the advantage of the communist states and their national liberation movement allies.[4]

David Funderburk's memoir of his time as US Ambassador to Bucharest (1981-5) confirms the success of Ceausescu's courtship of US administrations from Nixon to Reagan. The wise men of the State Department pursued their policy of "differentiation" between the various Warsaw Pact states with a dogged perseverance typical of the gullible who mistake themselves for the smart, and who dislike taking the advice of provincials. Unfortunately for him, Funderburk's background as a supporter of the conservative Senator, Jesse Helms, disqualified him from having an influence over US policy almost from the start of his ambassadorship – despite his knowledge of Romanian, his academic work on Romanian diplomatic history, and his previous visits to the country. Quite apart from what he has to say about US policy towards Ceausescu, Funderburk's book is a catalogue of the State Department's institutional weaknesses in dealing with Soviet bloc countries as a whole.[5]

Today, the results of Ceausescu's policies are increasingly apparent, despite 20 years of propaganda, coupled with the indifference of Western governments. Most of the claims made on behalf of his regime are being shown to be hollow. Far from modernising his country, his policies have impoverished it. But the current misery has been exacerbated by Western governments and institutions, convinced of Ceausescu's sincerity as an "independent" and "liberal", or believing that they could profit from co-operating with him. Whether cynical or deluded, such hopes are no longer widely held. The story of what has happened in Romania, and of how it was made possible, offers a sombre lesson – both for those who think that Western governments take human rights seriously, and perhaps even more for the proponents of a cynical foreign policy of self-interest.

II. Romanian Nightmares

Beneath the Bulldozer

"All politicians agree that when the people are too comfortable it is impossible to keep them within the bounds of their duty... They must be compared with mules, which, being used to burdens, are spoiled more by rest than labour" – Richelieu

The destruction of Bucharest's churches and cloisters seems to have struck a raw nerve in the West, perhaps because the destruction of its own architectural heritage is not yet entirely a thing of the past. Nonetheless, to seek to comprehend the enormity of Ceausescu's upheaval through comparisons with the activities of Western socialist town-planners and corrupt developers is to see events in Romania through a trivialising lense. Whatever the losses suffered by those uprooted from Britain's slums in the 1960s, and however soulless their new abodes, such people were not reduced to living on rations. The slum-dwellers' treatment was disgraceful, the motives behind it often criminal; but the municipal vandals did not force the urban population to rejoice at the demolition of their own homes.

Sensitivity to the destruction of beauty is certainly a virtue; and to bemoan the destruction of a nation's cultural inheritance is not merely "to pity the plumage and forget the dying bird." Within Romania itself, those who have risked raising their voices in criticism have emphasised the psychological and cultural torment aroused in them by the prospect of seeing ancient communities wiped from the face of the earth, and how it compounds and yet transcends the material and physical discomforts of everyday life. Whatever it was intended to do for the glory of the regime, the flattening of the centre of Bucharest began to draw the plight of its subjects to the West's attention. So too, many of the clichés around Ceausescu's name began to dissolve: for how could a "patriot" consign his nation's culture to the "rubbish heap of history"?

As Ceausescu's all-embracing programme of "systematisation, modernisation, civilisation" gathers pace, it creates a matchless sense of loss on the part of his subjects.[6] It is important to appreciate the radical nature of his plans. It is not intended to destroy only this or that neighbourhood in the cities, leaving others intact; nor to flatten only certain villages, while preserving others. Rather, the whole country is to be transformed into Ceausescu's vision of a communist society. Ceausescu's Marxist-Leninist beliefs have been consistently underrated. His sponsorship of the study of the ancient Dacians, and his repetitive assertion that Transylvania was always a Romanian territory, have often been presented as evidence that rabid nationalism has replaced communist ideals as the focus of legitimacy and intention on the part of his regime.

The dispute about whether the Romanians preceded the Magyars in the settlement of "the whole of Transylvania" also offers a classic example of the propagandist use of the past to serve the state's current purposes. In fact, the problem is an insoluble one, because of the paucity of reliable sources and the unreliability of historians. Along with everything else, scholarship has been nationalised in Romania – as in Hungary, though with fewer thoroughly disastrous academic consequences there. But the importance attached to it by Ceausescu has been underlined by the deployment of his own brother, Lieutenant-General

Ilie Ceausescu, to spearhead a campaign to uphold the official line. His volume, *Transylvania – An Ancient Romanian Land*, like any other book on this subject, quotes brother Nicolae on the "autochthonous" nature of the Romanian people: "They did not come from elsewhere, they did not fall down from the sky; they were born and lived here, in this land, and they defended it with their blood."[7] Even in the British press, bizarre advertisements have been carried alerting the British public to the official Romanian view of the controversy.[8]

Romania is not, however, the only communist state to be obsessed with asserting the antiquity of its rights and the inviolability of its frontiers, not least of those with its socialist brother-states. The recent disputes between East Germany and Poland over the definition of their border at sea is just the latest case in point. In another context, the Khmer Rouge, perhaps understandably, devoted much of their propaganda during the years of mayhem in Cambodia to asserting the sovereignty of "Democratic Kampuchea" .

Much of the Western media's coverage of Ceausescu's "systematisation" has tended to concentrate on the fate of the ethnic communities in Transylvania. Of course, the areas in which Romania's two million-strong Hungarian minority live will be devastated. Some ancient villages have already gone in the Szekler country, as have Saxon villages near Sibiu (Hermannstadt) and Brasov (Kronstadt). If Ceausescu's object were merely to break up the cohesion of troublesome ethnic minorities, by destroying their homes and redistributing them among the majority population, where they might more easily be controlled, then the "systematisation" could perhaps be described, despite its barbarity, as "rational" – at least in comparison with the actions of an ancient Assyrian conqueror. But it goes far beyond any such cruel reasoning.

Socialist justice can be even-handed. Since the bulk of the rural population is Romanian-speaking, the great majority of villages which will be ploughed under are inhabited purely by Romanians. Ceausescu's determination to put an end to the "ancient" Romanian presence in so many villages and hamlets in Transylvania, and throughout the rest of the country, gives the lie to his bombastic claims. As his bulldozers crush homes, churches and graveyards, and special secret police detachments of the *Securitate* herd the population away to "agro-industrial centres", Ceausescu's *völkisch* phrase-mongering reads only as hollow, ironic mockery:

> "In the toughest times, their forefathers did not desert the land where they were born, but, in brotherhood with it, with the mountains, fields, rivers and great woods, they unflinchingly remained in these parts, defending their being, their right to free existence."[9]

It is too early to say whether the initial onslaught has met with any resistance from the peasants. There has been talk among Hungarian peasants of acts of self-immolation, using the butane gas bottles which are the common source of fuel for cooking and heating in the countryside. In at least one Saxon settlement, it is reported that people sought sanctuary in the village church, only to be dragged out by special security troops. Fortified churches, which defied the Tatars and Turks, present no serious obstacle to Ceausescu's police. If the experience of Bucharest is any measure, Ceausescu's men will have no scruples about demolishing buildings with their inhabitants still inside – if, by their refusal to co-operate, they threaten to delay the schedule.[10]

Ceausescu's architectural gigantomania, and the ruthlessness of his plans, have led observers to compare his current policies with Hitler's ambitions to rebuild Berlin and cover an ever-expanding Greater German Reich with monuments to himself. Both in the out-size scale of their design and in their monotony, the buildings of the so-called "Civic Centre" in Bucharest are Hitlerian in dimension and spirit. It is hardly surprising that copies of Albert Speer's memoirs circulate clandestinely in Romania, as people try to fathom the mind of their ruler.[11] When he initiated the demolitions in the centre of Bucharest during the summer of 1984, Ceausescu proclaimed a millenial vision worthy of comparison with Hitler's vision of the political message conveyed by architecture:

> "Today, I have inaugurated the task of building the House of the Republic and the Boulevard of the Victory of Socialism, the grandiose and luminous foundations of this epoch of profound transformations and innovations, of monumental buildings which will persist across the ages."[12]

Albert Speer concluded that, in order to fulfill his plans to transform Berlin and other cities in his empire, Hitler had to be intent on conquest, so that he could exploit the raw materials and forced labour of subject peoples. Since the option of foreign conquest, as a means of subsidising his mania for "systematisation", has not been open to Ceausescu, he has been driven, of necessity, to exploit his own people. The fact that inauguration of the long-awaited "systematisation" coincided with an ever-worsening external trade and debt crisis simply intensified the drainage of resources from purposes serving the well-being of the people. Not since the archaic civilisations of ancient Egypt and the Near East have rulers imposed such burdens upon their own subjects. Even then, however, the pharoahs built their pyramids in the desert – not on the homes of their subjects.

The Cult of Industrialisation

Despite the similarity of their appearance, it would be a mistake to compare Ceausescu's urban projects only with the schemes of Hitler, or with the new towns and prestige buildings of Mussolini. Of course, they have much in common; but the Soviet model should not be overlooked. The notion of transforming the environment, as well as the urban landscape, has a long tradition in communist thought. Whatever his criticisms of the capitalist economic system, Marx could not find enough praise for the bourgeoisie's conquest of nature and development of modern technology. The cult of industrialisation, and its identification as a prerequisite of communist rule, which was central to Lenin's thought, was given expression in his slogan, "communism = Soviet power, plus the electrification of the whole country." Nor was it only Stalin's supporters who advocated rapid industrialisation and forced urbanisation. If anything, Trotsky's dreams when still in power were more extreme. For Trotsky, the revolution would be followed by a conquest of nature so complete that shifting the features of the landscape would be no more trouble than moving furniture around a room. Khrushchev, similarly, was a leading figure in the vandalisation of Moscow, and of so many churches and monasteries, both at Stalin's instigation and in his own right.[13] Today, the Soviet regime has retreated from some of the hubristic schemes of the past – like its plan to divert the course of the rivers of Siberia. But it is the Bolshevik dream of the early years which Ceausescu is now set upon fulfilling in Romania.

Romanian propaganda delights in describing the country's enormous civil engineering projects. Tunnels and viaducts for new highways have been built without thought for the petrol-rationing. The Danube-Black Sea Canal was completed four years ago, but is running at only about 10 per cent of its potential capacity. Unperturbed by the failure of international traffic to make use of the already completed network of navigable waterways, the Romanian government plans to link Bucharest to the Danube with a new canal.[14]

The inadequacy of command economy planning has been repeatedly revealed over the last 40 years of Romanian history. By the 1970s, for instance, although Romania's own oil-fields were no longer able to meet domestic demand, its refining capacity was already built up beyond domestic needs. When the Iranian revolution and subsequent Gulf War limited supplies of crude for processing and further sale, while forcing the price of oil to unprecedented heights, Romania was faced with a severe problem. The petroleum products imported from the Soviet Union now had to be paid for in hard currency nearer to the world market price. At the same time, much of Romania's refining capacity in so far as it had ever existed, lay idle because of the decline in foreign demand.

The bizarre history of Romania's warship-building programme offers another example of the regime's pursuit of unrealistic goals. Having scrapped the Romanian fleet in 1967, probably because its submarines and destroyers were of greater use as auxiliaries in Soviet war plans than for Romanian purposes, the decision was taken, sometime in the later 1970s, to build up a maritime industry with powerful warships. Given its base in the Black Sea, the only likely opponent of Ceausescu's growing naval power is the Soviet navy, which could dispose of his fleet in short order. Attempts to explain rationally the massive investments required to develop a naval ship-building capacity usually concentrate on the possibility of exporting vessels to other states. But a study of this episode – peculiar even by Ceausescu's standards – leads to the conclusion that, since the design of the Romanian warships is based on outdated Soviet and Chinese models, and since their weaponry and electronic intelligence systems are likely to be just as dated, there can be little chance of selling them – even to Third World leaders as obsessed with prestige as Ceausescu himself. If the new navy has been constructed to protect Romania's barely exploited off-shore oil interests with a largely notional mercantile marine, then both the navy and the dockyards built for it have been a monumental waste of money.[15]

The rural "systematisation" programme itself not only flies in the face of morality and reason, but also defies the recent experience of Romanian agriculture. Even at the risk of a breach with Moscow, and with the strategy agreed upon by the other Comecon states, Ceausescu insisted on continuing the Stalinist drive for all-round industrialisation and urbanisation which had been begun by Gheorghiu-Dej. Agriculture was persistently neglected, and the peasantry were encouraged, often obliged, to become urban industrial workers. Western observers applauded Ceausescu's "independent stance", and the "improvements" which he was making. At the same time, the harvest could only be brought in with the aid of army conscripts, students and school pupils.

Needless to say, the incentives to produce food have declined. The collective farms are at least as inefficient as those elsewhere, and the low official prices have discouraged production on private plots. The remedy for the unwillingness to produce for the state-regulated markets on private plots was the introduction of obligatory deliveries to the state sector, at the risk of losing the private plot if these were not made.[16]

The growing export of foodstuffs, in order to fund the development projects, and the import of machinery and petroleum products, are not the only cause of the shortages of food in Romania. The labour force employed in the harvesting has little agricultural experience, and even less incentive to work well. Furthermore, the system of collection, storage and distribution of foodstuffs – particularly grain and fresh vegetables – is notoriously inadequate and incompetent. According to estimates by the US Department of Agriculture, the real corn crop was 30 per cent below the reported output in 1985. In 1986, Ceausescu himself admitted that three of the 23 million tons harvested had been lost. Another estimate, published in Romania, put the total losses resulting from bad harvesting methods, poor transportation and storage at up to 45 per cent of the total.[17] Ceausescu's solution is to increase the area under cultivation by destroying more rural communities, even though the present acreage cannot be tilled properly. Instead of relying on local people to farm the land with care, it will be done by commuters from the agro-industrial centres – despite the official encouragement to make more use of horse-drawn vehicles to save petrol.

Modernism at Work

Party resolutions and laws promoting "territorial systematisation" date from 1967 and 1971.

Although they are only now being implemented, they should be seen as part of a long-term scheme. When he spoke on this theme to the "Fourth National Conference of the Chairman of People's Councils" in Bucharest, at the beginning of March 1988, Ceausescu "stressed the importance of the administrative reorganisation of the country 20 years ago... for the policy of rational distribution of the forces of production." He added that "in consideration of the fact that some counties and rural settlements had been depopulated", the time was ripe "to *radically wipe out* the major differences between towns and villages, to bring the working and living conditions of the working people in the countryside closer to those in the towns, to provide for the *harmonious* development of the whole country, to more powerfully *homogenise* our socialist society, to create a *single worker people*[sic]."[18]

At the end of April, in his address to the Political Executive Committee of the Romanian Communist Party, Ceausescu demanded "the expansion of the socialist farming system to encompass *all* the agriculture, to achieve within the agro-industrial councils ... the co-operation of the whole peasantry." The "agro-industrial councils" will be the economic administrative bodies for the newly "systematised" units. They will include the pastoral farmers from the hills and mountains ("I stress it again"); and they will thus complete the state control of agriculture. In the spring, Ceausescu was still evincing a mock moderation, declaring that "it is not necessary to rush things". But only five years were set for the completion of the planning and initial implementation stages; and the demolition of up to 8000 villages and hamlets was still being discussed blandly:

> "It is necessary to cut down to almost half the number of villages, establishing those that are to remain and their size; all new buildings shall have to be erected only in these localities and... we shall have to put other village areas to other purposes."[19]

The remaining 5–6000 villages will be grouped around the 558 "agro-industrial centres". Officially, it is planned to demolish 443,000 houses in the years 1986–90, and to build 725,000. It is easy to see which part of the plan is more likely to "overfulfilled".

The "homogenisation" of the population, to use one of Ceausescu's favourite terms, will be achieved by the relocation of the 5–8 million people who are to be displaced from the land and lodged in new housing. But up to 10 million people will be directly affected.[20] The former peasants' new homes will be in blocks of flats; and there will be little to distinguish one from another anywhere in the country. *Romanian News* carried an interview with Stefan Datcu, one of the official architects, in which the uniformity of the building plans was extolled:

> "The designing of [internal] spaces is in keeping with a unitary legislation. The living room, the bedrooms, the bathroom, the rooms' height and other dimensions are therefore the *same in a small or a big town*."[21]

In short, no two kitchens will be different. Everyone will be equal.

Such equality is guaranteed by the pre-fabricated concrete slabs which will provide the shells of the new blocks. The new buildings are narrowly concentrated, usually in the centre of a "surviving" village. Alexandru Lazarescu, the deputy director of the State Planning Committee, has admitted that "attention has been paid to reducing building lots, so that the new projects may be sited *only in the heart of villages* with a high construction density."[22] In reality, many of these blocks will lack basic amenities, such as running water above ground level. Frequently, as many as six families will have to share one kitchen and bathroom. The new style of life will facilitate the surveillance of the population, since under such conditions it will be difficult to preserve any privacy whatsoever. It will also be difficult to keep pigs, goats and other animals, let alone to grow vegetables.

Even with the most tortuous logic possible, it is hard to share Ceausescu's joyful anticipation of the forthcoming "abolition of the distinction between town and country", nor his incredulity that "now, when the Romanian people are experiencing happiness... one cannot understand people who wish to leave their country."[23] Even official publications disseminating propaganda abroad reveal a wistful sense of loss on the part of those obliged to celebrate the "reconstruction" of their home towns. But all of these schemes reveal a dogmatic insistence upon the need to transform Romania into a "modern" and "developed" – and socialist – society. The conception of what is "modern", which has dictated developments, is so crudely primitive that it would be laughable were it not the root cause of so much suffering. Yet it is this brutal "modernism" which is the hallmark of "scientific socialism". From the old-world comfort of former royal palaces and hunting lodges, Ceausescu envisages a jungle of reinforced concrete, of "homogenisation", of conformity and primitive industrial squalor; and he calls it "the most just social system mankind has ever known."[24]

Sacrificing a Generation

The costs of all such schemes to transform Romania have been borne by the ordinary people. Western credits have not eased their burdens. On the contrary, the supply of funds and technology, along with the continuing access to Western markets, has encouraged the regime in its intention to push ahead with its policies as rapidly as possible. Even when difficulties over debt repayments and further loans became acute in the early 1980s, the preferred solution was to cut back on the standard of living and consumer goods rather than to rein in the more ambitious and absurd projects. By 1988, the Romanian people had been subject to at least 20 years of forced accumulation, with 30 per cent of the national income, on average, being devoted annually to investment in projects of dubious viability. Prior to the first great oil shock of 1973–4, the standard of living *in the towns* may have shown some improvement over the terrible years of collectivisation in the 1950s, when Ceausescu was one of the chief enforcers of Dej's policy. By the later 1970s, however, the problems were already becoming apparent. Even before the fall of the Shah, the shortages – which have since worsened remorselessly – were already leading to episodic and localised crises of supply. Citrus fruits, for example, had long been unobtainable, as elsewhere in the Soviet bloc.

Since 1983, the rationing of foodstuffs has been the norm. Currently, each Romanian is entitled to a daily ration of 300–500 grammes of bread, in addition to a monthly ration of one and a half kilos of maize, 300 grammes of butter *or* cheese, and four kilos of potatoes. Only Cuban sugar is allocated in relatively generous proportions, at 1.2 kilos per month. At the Party Conference in December 1987, Ceausescu offered a New Year bonus of a guaranteed 30 grammes of poultry per week.[25] Of course, the possession of coupons does not really guarantee access to the goods in question. Nor can the quality of the rationed foodstuffs be regarded as acceptable, even to a population accustomed to a revolution of diminishing expectations.

Electricity and gas supplies have also been restricted by government decree. A maximum of one 40-watt light bulb is permitted in any room. Posters proclaiming draconian penalties for the misuse of electricity were on display in the forecourts of housing blocks in Bucharest last winter. Even "luxury class" hotel rooms are restricted to a couple of dim lamps. Naturally, these energy-saving measures are felt most acutely in the winter. In 1987, the winter was relatively mild; but the two previous winters were bitterly cold. The combination of power-cuts and the cold weather led to an unspecified number of deaths, especially among the elderly and very young. Some people also adopted the risky and sometimes fatal habit of sleeping in their kitchens. Although they could hope to maximise the benefit of a minimal and all-purpose use of fuel, they exposed themselves to the risk of asphyxiation if they fell asleep leaving their gas-stoves on, only for there to be a cut in the gas-supply during the night, followed by its resumption.[26]

Under-the-counter deals in shops and peasant markets have become the norm; so those with something tangible to offer can, to some extent, circumvent food-rationing. As in any society, the effects of rationing are felt most severely by the elderly, who tend also to be the poorest. Some pensioners are able to supplement their pitiful allowances by standing in queues, in return for tips from people who are still in work and unable to take time off while the shops are open. Unskilled workers, and people like school teachers with no control over exam results, have little muscle in such a distorted market-place. The energy regulations are enforced by crude price mechanisms, involving swingeing surcharges for anyone using more than the statutory maximum. Here again, it is those in need who are the most penalised. The object of the energy-saving policy is not, after all, a social, but a crudely economic one – to sustain the viability of policies which have had such negative consequences. The ratchet effect is only worsened by energy conservation.

It is not only at home that Romanians suffer from the crude implementation of this austerity programme. There are well-authenticated cases of factories suddenly losing their electricity supply in the course of production, despite the damage done to machinery, and of coal-miners left underground by power-cuts.[27] The loss of productive capacity caused by the arbitrary restricting of electricity in industry is difficult to quantify; but it must be considerable. Indeed, it is baffling that anyone professing concern with a systematic and orderly plan of production could authorise them. The loss of power in hospitals during operations, or in intensive care and incubation wards, has also been reported frequently. The regime is doing its best to discourage longevity among those too old to work, and those over 60 years of age are regularly refused expensive medical treatment, whether in hospital or through medications. It is a practice which makes gruesome sense to a government bending every effort to fulfil its plan. But for a government anxious to increase the population from 23 to 30 million by the end of the century, the willing sacrifice of infants is a cruel self-contradiction.[28]

The schemes to boost the birthrate typify the intrusion of the party into the most personal spheres of life. Official publications emphasise that "population growth is no longer a spontaneous phenomenon in Romania."[29] In 1985, "demographic command units" were introduced to enforce plans to rectify the situation. Their prime duty was to force women between the age of puberty and their mid-forties to undergo monthly gynaecological examinations designed to ensure their fertility. From February 1986, only women who had had five or more children were released from such extreme instrusions into their privacy. From 1965 until 1984, the natural rate of increase in the population fell continuously, from 6.0 to 3.87 per 1,000. But it is not difficult to pinpoint the obstacles to an increase in the birthrate. In addition to the shortages of medical supplies and food – especially of fresh milk – overcrowding and decline in the quality of housing militate against the plan's success. It is yet another example of the brutal primitivism evident in the regime's aims. Despite his claims to be a moderniser, numbers alone count for Ceausescu.[30]

Contraceptives are virtually unobtainable; and abortion has been all but outlawed. Since 1985, when the anti-abortion law of 1966 was strengthened, a mother has been able to obtain an abortion only in exceptional circumstances: if the mother's life is endangered; if the foetus is likely to be physically or mentally disabled; if the mother is over 45; if she has already had five children; or in cases of rape or incest. Despite this, there were more abortions than live births until as late as 1983, the last year for which official figures were available. Ceausescu himself claimed that only nine per cent had genuine medical justifications. Of course, he neglected to consider the declining health of Romanian women. A report at the beginning of 1985 revealed the horrifying fact that only five per cent of 200,000 women surveyed in Bucharest had a healthy uterus. The widespread resort to abortion, often performed in illegal and gruesome circumstances, must be the principal cause of this. The black market is dominant in this area too, but with less beneficial effects than in food distribution.[31]

The grim realities of everyday life in Romania seem set to worsen steadily. It is unlikely that the coming winter will be as mild as the last. It may, indeed, be just as severe as the previous two. Tens of thousands of people are likely to find themselves housed more poorly than ever before. Their cottages will have been destroyed by the bulldozers; but their new accommodation will be unfinished or inadequate. Food and heating will, if anything, be in shorter supply than before. The tragic consequences for the very young, the elderly and the weak are easily predictable.

Perhaps Ceausescu truly believes that, after all these sacrifices, everything will turn out to have been for the best in a couple of decades or so. Perhaps he would also echo Stalin's comment about the human cost of the first two Five Year Plans, made to Churchill in Moscow in 1942 – "What is one generation?"[32] Seeing the problems facing the Soviet Union or China today, however, after more than one generation of "great helmsmen", no independent observer can be optimistic about the results of investing so much in infrastructure, as the very basis of existence is undermined. But these tremendous projects, and the disproportionate sacrifices which they demand from the population, have undoubtedly served a key political purpose: they have degraded the population to below the level at which protest or resistance are viable. Daily survival and daily labour demand far too much energy for that.

III. High Stalinism in Action

Protests and Promises

"Let them hate so long as they fear" – Caligula

It is clear that there are good grounds for widespread discontent with the Romanian regime. What is less clear, however, is how much dissent, let alone outright opposition, exists, and whether any kind of critical organisation is possible under current conditions. Leaving aside the organs of Ceausescu's authority, the multi-ethnic composition and religious divisions of Romania's population, as well as its common history and experiences, have all combined to make organised, widespread and effective resistance to the regime impossible thus far. For a decade after the miners' strike in the Jiu valley in 1977, the apparent quiescence of the population seemed to justify the critical accusations of passivity which could be heard not only in the West, but also among dissidents elsewhere in the Soviet bloc.

Glib assertions are often made, not only with regard to the Romanians, that since "they" have never had liberty, they do not miss it; and that since "they" have become accustomed to privations over the centuries, they do not notice new shortages. No one would deny that Romanian history has taught sombre lessons, even for the most optimistic. But in domestic, historical terms, the situation under communist rule is unprecedented. The Tatars were ruthless and rapacious; but their raids were only intermittent. The Turks mulcted the population; but they did not try to transform them. Even Vlad Dracul's famous penchant for impaling was inflicted principally on foreign enemies. There are, however, parallels to what is going on in Romania today in the histories of every other communist state. Romania is unusual only for going through its Stalin phase twice – though the whole communist period, since the consolidation of communist power in 1947, should perhaps be seen as an era of "high Stalinism".

No country under "real existing socialism" has yet seen a successful counter-revolution from within against the Communist Party's rule without foreign assistance. Some regimes have been threatened more seriously than others. But it is striking how even such an unpopular and derided regime as that of Poland was able to find the resources in police and military might to suppress the Solidarity movement. General Jaruzelski's coup in December 1981 was aided and prompted by the Soviet Union; but the martial law regime which it imposed was based on Polish manpower. The near disintegration of the party in Poland had not affected its hold over the police and armed forces to the same degree. Despite their almost complete alienation from Polish society, and even from the bulk of card-carrying party members, Jaruzelski's military supporters have been able to prolong the viability of the regime to a degree which few people inside or outside Poland could have expected.

The Polish example is important for several reasons. First, the Poles are often held up as an example for the Romanians to follow, and as one which Ceausescu must fear. Attempts to prevent Poles from travelling to Romania, and the restrictions placed on contacts with them by the Romanian authorities, clearly indicate that the risk of contagion is taken very seriously. Despite the similar economic miseries existing in Poland and Romania, however, the example of Solidarity will not be an easy one to copy. Ceausescu and his organs of authority may have taken comfort from the apparent success of the post- December 1981 regime in Poland. In the early 1980s, it may even have encouraged him to press on with his "all-round" economic programme, confident of being able to control any resulting tensions.

The disorders in Brasov in November 1987 brought the discontent of the industrial workforce of Romania briefly into the world's headlines and seemed to rouse the spectre of organised working class opposition – the ultimate fear of any socialist regime. The spontaneous and disorganised character of the revolt ensured that, after the satisfaction of ransacking the local party headquarters and revealing the privileged life-style of its inhabitants, the demonstrators were easily dispersed by riot police and other special forces. But despite the ease with which order was restored, and the lack of serious violence on the part of the demonstrators (though not on the part of the police), the riots clearly sent shock-waves through Romania. Even the official news agency, *Agerpress*, admitted that "deeds... alien to the socialist system" had been committed by "some elements of the workforce", who had thereby "injured the honour of the collective." As a result, about 300 troublemakers were "expelled from the collective", whilst the managing director of the "Red Flag" truck factory was sacked, along with the entire management team.[33]

The postponement of the Communist Party conference in December 1987 may have been a result of the discontent made evident in Brasov. Rumours about Ceausescu's ill-health, which surfaced as a reason for the delay in assembling the delegates, may have been true; or they may have been a diversionary tactic to distract attention from the real cause. Whatever the reason, however, Ceausescu felt obliged to confess to the "errors" committed by others, not by himself, and to promise improvements in the supply of basic foodstuffs. Since these promises have not been kept, they were, after all, perhaps nothing more than ritual declarations of a better tomorrow. On the other hand, since they came in Ceausescu's second speech to the Conference, after a typically uncompromising opening speech, it would appear that some form of verbal concession was being made to those anxious about the situation behind the scenes.[34]

The Strings of Power

Superficially, the open expression of discontent by the workers of the "Red Flag" factory at Brasov seemed to resemble Polish events under the declining Gierek regime. They were outraged by a combination of shortages, wage reductions and effective price increases, as well as by the threat of "relocation" – or dismissal – if they failed to fulfil the norms prescribed by the plan. The threat posed not only to Ceausescu's rule, but also to the authority of the Communist Party itself, was assessed in an unusual public statement issued by the veteran communist, Silviu Brucan, at the end of November 1987. Clearly, the Polish example was in the forefront of Brucan's mind:

> "A period of crisis has opened up in the relationship between the Communist Party and the working class... We have seen in Poland what such a rupture means and how difficult it is for the Party to regain the confidence of the workers, *even when the best of intentions to improve their lot is apparent.*"[35]

Brucan, a one-time Romanian ambassador to Washington, was briefly put under house arrest for his pains. His lenient treatment – in comparison with that of the Brasov strikers, many of whom were sentenced to forced labour – was probably due to the fact that he had avoided placing any blame upon the *Conducator* personally. Brucan is the nearest equivalent, in Romanian terms, to that phenomenon of the Brezhnev years, the "official dissident." Nonetheless, he was sufficiently alarmed by the situation to be prepared to overstep the narrow bounds of official indulgence. He saw that the threat posed by the alienation of the working class was a threat to the communist system itself, and not just to the current leadership. Furthermore, his analysis of the basic mechanisms underlying the leadership's power was revealing, and at variance with the Western view that Romania is merely a "police state."

As an experienced Marxist-Leninist, Brucan knows that the real basis of authority in a communist state lies with the party, not with the state security apparatus. This is as true of Romania as it is of other communist states – *pace* those interest-group analysts who distinguish the KGB, for instance, from the party in the Soviet Union. Naturally, Brucan chose to express the truth of the power-relationship in an ideologically acceptable way:

> "I must take issue with a misconception prevailing in the West that this regime owes its survival to the repressive organs of the state. Surely this could not explain more than two decades of political stability. In fact, *the main instrument of power has been the Communist Party*, with security forces playing only a marginal role and dealing with especially deviant cases."[36]

Paul Goma, the *emigre* poet, described this phenomenon in 1977, in a letter to the Czech dissident, Pavel Kohout: "You live under Russian occupation; we Romanians live under Romanian occupation, more efficient than a foreign one."[37]

Nobody would deny the fear which is inspired by the *Securitate*, nor the grounds for it; but what makes it effective is its collaboration with the party network. The party's members provide many regular informers, who back up the full-time officials of the state security apparatus. But it is the party itself which is the information-gathering and disciplinary body *par excellence* in Romania.

Of course, "democratic centralism" ensures that the vast majority of party members fulfil their functions as transmission belts for the commands of the centre. Whether their role as providers of information for the centre's decision-making process is as reliable, however, must be doubted. As elsewhere in the Soviet bloc, careers are not made by relaying unpalatable news to the leader. In the late 1960s and early 1970s, Ceausescu carried through radical reforms in the relationship between local party bosses and the centre, and between the party and state organs. In effect, the state apparatus was subordinated to the party at each level, normally by placing party and state positions in the same hands. Since Ceausescu, as Secretary General, already dominated day-to-day promotions and methods of discipline within the party, these reforms played a vital part in the complete subordination of party, state and society to his will. Over his 23 years in office, Ceausescu's domination of the party has steadily increased, aided by his wife's assumption of control over cadre policy.

This process of *perestroika* was accompanied, however, by a brief period of literary freedom, when there was open criticism of the pre-Ceausescu period (though Ceausescu himself had been a member of Gheorghiu-Dej's Politburo), and veiled criticism of the Soviet Union. It seems to have encouraged the widespread Western illusion that Ceausescu's administrative reforms, and the still-greater concentration of authority in the hands of the party leadership, were somehow a liberalising measure.[38] The assumption seems to have been a simple one: Ceausescu had revealed himself to be a kind of closet "liberal" by his unenthusiastic reaction to the Brezhnev Doctrine, and he was undoubtedly a "nationalist"; so any extension of his power at the expense of the "old Stalinists" in the provinces should be welcomed.

To enhance his authority over the party, Ceausescu has also used the tactic of enlarging its various bodies, to make them unwieldy and ineffective as anything other than claques. The RCP's 3.5 million members make it proportionately the largest Communist Party in Europe. More importantly, the re-division of the country into 40 counties from the original 16 after 1967 helped to reduce the power of the local bosses in relation to the centre, just as their authority over their own fiefs was increased through the combination of state and party functions. The size of the Central Committee and Politburo has also grown under Ceausescu, thus reducing their effectiveness as potential centres of discussion. In addition, the rapid turnover in the membership of such bodies, as in the ministerial seats of the government, has reduced the likelihood of any opposition faction within the party leadership, let alone of a faction capable of ousting the Secretary General, as the apparently loyal Khrushchevites removed their own First Secretary in October 1964.[39]

In the mid-1980s, newspaper reporters and academic experts grew confident that Ceausescu's days as a leader were numbered, and that the *fin de regime* was already imminent. It seemed obvious that within the leadership of the party, state security and military apparatus there must be men who could see the consequences of Ceausescu's policies, and who would seek, out of pure self-interest, to oust Ceausescu and his clan before it was too late – wanting neither to inherit an impoverished under-developing country, nor to be blamed for their part in its pauperisation. But their rational assumptions were inappropriate. Perhaps the secret behind the failure of any internal coup lies with the adamantine strength of Ceausescu's hold over the strings of power – through his combination of standard "democratic centralist" techniques, backed up by his deployment of clan members at key points in the party-state apparatus. For instance, not only does Elena Ceausescu control overall cadre policy, but within the Ministry of Interior, her husband's brother (also named Nicolae by their somewhat unimaginative parents) heads the "cadres department". Periodic reports of attempted military coups have probably been merely the exaggerated outcome of disciplinary actions against army officers, muttering in their cups about being degraded to the level of uniformed farm-workers and navvies.[40]

In addition to the reinforcing effects of "socialism in one family", the charismatic hold of Ceausescu's personality over the tiny elite should not be underrated. Clearly, he is not a fool like Gierek; nor is he likely to let things get out of hand without firing a shot. However corrupt his minions may be – and their plundering of the country would astonish the most jaundiced observer – they too have learnt a lesson from Gierek's squabbling and disintegrating band. Whatever rivalries and ambitions exist within the elite, they know that if they do not hang together, they will certainly hang separately. If they fall out with each other, the release of pressure from below may well lead to an uncontrollable explosion.[41]

In short, desperate power-struggles may be raging behind the scenes; but on past evidence, they are struggles between those seeking Ceausescu's favour, rather than those seeking to supplant him. At the same time, intervention from a "reformist" Soviet leadership looks less and less likely. But even if it is accepted that the regime cannot be overthrown – or even radically modified – from below, other than through the exploitation of divisions within the RCP leadership and as a result of external pressure, should this necessarily lead to the sombre conclusion that dissent and resistance on the part of the subject population are futile?

Clearly, the open incitement of rebellion, and open acts of resistance against the military forces and secret police units of the regime, can only be noble folly. They are likely to occur in individual localities, as the general grievances of the population are ignited by specific instances of oppression and mismanagement. But unless there is a collapse of discipline, they will be forcibly suppressed. The troops and police at the disposal of the government cannot fail to be affected themselves by the shortages, and by the general climate of misery; but the officer corps, and particularly the *Securitate* and front-line riot-control units, enjoy material privileges which set them apart from the rest of the population. In this way, they form a closed network, like that of the riot police and army officers who made the imposition of martial law possible in Poland. Like Jaruzelski, Ceausescu also gained direct experience of the methods of maintaining ideological and political control over these forces earlier in his career.[42]

Collaboration and Silent Resistance

Romania lacks the peculiar mixture of factors which made the aspirations of Solidarity so plausible in Poland in 1980, and which have preserved the identity of Polish society in opposition to the state. Romania has some of the same sources of discontent. But what welded the Polish people into an enormous mass movement was not just the uniformly desperate economic outlook: that was the pre-condition of discontent. It was also the existence of an independent Church and Polish Pope, who between them had the loyalty of the vast majority of the population. Furthermore, the Church co-operated with intellectuals and would-be trade unionists in providing facilities for meetings and other essential elements of organisation. Most of all, it provided a haven from the party's domination and interference in every other sphere of life.

None of these conditions exists in Romania. The Romanian population is ethnically diverse – in addition to two million Hungarians and approximately 200,000 Germans, there are also Slovaks, Serbs and Jews, and an unknown number of gypsies. Religious divisions are sharp, and cut across ethnic lines, complicating the picture. The great bulk of professing ethnic Romanians are Orthodox, although some in Transylvania belong to the Uniate branch of the Catholic Church. This was made illegal in 1948 after Stalin had taken the lead by outlawing the Ukrainian Uniates. Recently, however, there have been signs of increasing official tolerance of Uniates who use the Romanian language in their services. This offers some means of dividing the Catholic community along ethnic lines, of facilitating control over those elements which were previously underground, and of isolating the Hungarian-speaking Uniates.[43] Many of the Hungarians are Calvinists, although some are Catholic Uniates. The Siebenbürger Germans are generally Evangelical, whereas the Swabians of the Banat are usually Catholic.

The Orthodox Church enjoys an unwritten agreement with the regime: in return for docility, and for preaching obedience, it is left unpersecuted. But it is not left undisturbed. Its churches and monasteries are also major victims of "systematisation". The Orthodox hierachy, however, is unwilling to endanger its limited rights by protesting openly. Instead, it collaborates in order to "preserve what is left to the Church" and confines itself to the liturgical aspects of its many responsibilities. Entry into the priesthood and promotion within the hierarchy are controlled by the party; and even the Patriarch's ecumenical contacts are subject to surveillance by the *Securitate*. Individual Orthodox priests and monks have taken issue with the regime over its policies; but their voices have been silenced, without any intervention on the part of the hierarchy.[44]

The other churches are still more exposed to police interference; and none possesses the facilities to act as a rallying point for the preservation of a pan-Romanian, non-communist spirit. There appears to be a revival of interest in religion, particularly in the form of charismatic sects; but these are not able to constitute an integrating force on a broad scale. They are also persecuted for their faith. Even the remaining Jewish minority, whose treatment has been cited as exemplary within the Soviet bloc, has been repeatedly subjected to anti-semitic abuse in the official media.[45]

The regime has also attempted to exploit long-standing national feuds among the ethnic groups to facilitate its control. To some extent, this has been successful; but there is a growing impression among *Romanian-speakers* themselves that Romanian nationalism is becoming much less easy to incite. On the other hand, a relatively privileged dissident from the Hungarian minority, Karoly Kiraly, has advised his fellow Magyars against using their ethnic solidarity as a basis for mass disobedience. Kiraly fears that the government would be able to divert Romanian discontent into hostility towards the minorities.[46] The steady emigration of Germans since 1978 has also helped to isolate the Hungarians. Few Germans with the prospect of an exit visa have any incentive to mar their own records. Members of both minorities have taken part in demonstrations, in most cases resulting from the release of anger at the time of the Brasov events; but even then, they have been reluctant to identify themselves as Hungarians or Germans in the chanting of slogans and other expressions of discontent.

Just as the Romanian churches are not able to offer a focus of national identity and resistance to the "transformations" demanded by the government, so too the intellectuals have not managed to form any organisation on the model of the Polish KOR, Committee for the Defence of the Workers. An attempt to form a free trade union, in February 1979, was suppressed, as have been any subsequent efforts in the same direction.[47] Romanian intellectuals, as a group, have come in for a great deal of criticism, not least because so many of them welcomed Ceausescu's apparent "opening up" of the bounds of official tolerance at the end of the 1960s. His criticism of the invasion of Czechoslovakia also brought him cheap popularity. Many who, at that time, sang his praises have since lived to change their tune – but under conditions in which their voices are hardly likely to reach a mass audience.

The workers and peasants of Romania have tended to treat the intellectuals with suspicion. When Silviu Brucan claims that the 1960s were good years for the ordinary people, his argument does not seem unreasonable:

"The party could successfully control the mass of workers because it became popular in the 1960s, when a turn for the better occurred... in the standard of living of almost three million peasants who joined the urban industrial workforce. There was plenty of food, and there was no comparison with the 'idiocy of rural life' which they had left behind."[48]

Bourgeois intellectuals, it seems, especially those with Marxist convictions, are better judges of what is good for the peasants than the peasants themselves. The history of Twentieth Century developments is a catalogue of the imposition of values and practices on the unwilling rural poor, whose whole style of life has been shattered. Given the sort of shoddy housing into which the rural influx was already being herded by the 1960s, it is probably more accurate to see it as a first stage in "systematisation" than as a breakthrough in the quality of life – although no one anticipated what life would be like in the "Golden Age" 20 years later. They were evidently too poor and uneducated to share the illusions of their betters.

The intelligentsia – in its broad sense, including white collar workers as well as writers and academics – operates in controlled conditions. Academic institutes, like every other place of work, have security officers attached to them who keep tabs on visitors. Since 1983, for example, typewriters have had to be registered with the *Securitate*. In addition, needless to say, only official institutions may possess photocopiers – and few do. The production of *samizdat* material is, therefore, at least as hazardous as anywhere else in Eastern Europe, and more technically difficult. Illegal pamphlets and leaflets do appear from time to time; but no regular underground journals appear to have succeeded in establishing themselves. The various inducements to inform are no less effective among the intellectuals than among other social groups.

There have been recurrent reports of student discontent, together with expressions of solidarity with the striking workers in Brasov. But as with most news about opposition inside Romania, the details are sketchy. They reveal two apparently contradictory trends: first, that discontent is only expressed openly in a patchy way; and second, that discontent among workers and students is, nevertheless, widespread. Given the severe and often brutal punishments meted out for organising meetings or distributing material critical of official policies, let alone critical the person of the *Conducator*, it could hardly be otherwise.

In a more general sense, much of Romanian society is in a permanent state of low-intensity strike. The failure to fulfil work norms and the circumvention of official guidelines, along with the resort to the black market, are all forms of relatively low-risk resistance.

Refusing to attend party or works council meetings to celebrate official anniversaries is another way of expressing displeasure, which goes beyond the otherwise ubiquitous attitude in Eastern Europe – "they pretend to pay us, so we pretend to work."[49]

Despite the reprisals taken against those who vote against the official candidates in elections, Romania has a surprisingly high rate of "no" votes or spoilt ballots. At the last general election, on 17 March 1985, the turnout was officially put at 99.99 per cent; but the candidates of the Socialist Democracy and Unity Front received only 97.3 per cent of the votes. Since 1969, when only 0.2 per cent of the voters rejected the SDUF slate, according to official figures, there has been a substantial rise in those prepared to run the risks of a public expression of discontent.[50]

The daily struggle for existence, however, has helped to drain much of the energy which might otherwise have gone into protest activities. Even young people seem to engage in little of the aimless hooliganism which has become a normal expression of the anomy of life in the less hysterical socialist states. Life is so poor that issues like the drastic pollution of the environment, and the grave deficiency of food and drink, play a less significant role in Romania than elsewhere in Eastern Europe. Rumours abounded of the horrific consequences for local people, as well as wildlife, of the leak of toxic waste which occurred at Sulina in the Danube Delta in July 1988. But the real source of these problems – the irresponsibility of the government for the welfare of the public – meant that protest was futile. As with all other grievances, this extreme case was just another result of Ceausescu's "cult of personality."[51] *Romanian Democratic Action*, a dissident group about which little is known (which probably accounts for its survival since 1985), sent a report to the Austrian Foreign Minister, Alois Mock, on the pollution of the Romanian environment, which rejected the Marxist idea of dominating, exploiting and transforming Man and nature.[52]

Not even official propaganda can entirely disguise the distorting effects of living in a society under constant observation by the organs of state security. *Romania Today*, for example, carried a report about a science fiction story, "The White City", by a 12-year-old schoolgirl, which might well have been taken for a thinly veiled satire on Romanian reality if it had not been selected for such praise:

> "Liliana Cojocaru creates a huge urban settlement, which initiates mankind's good and peaceful actions, a kind of general headquarters of quiet and security. Extra-sensitive radars are continually detecting not only tensions among countries and peoples anywhere on Earth, *but also the smallest disputes among friends, or even among parents and children.*"[53]

Ceausescu knows as well as de Tocqueville that revolutions come about when despotic governments abandon tyranny and seek to reform themselves. Constant pressure downwards is as much a political imperative as an ideological necessity. For many people, family life and its obligations are a means of denying the regime its demands. The obligation to applaud can still, at least, be ignored at home. But "systematisation" will not only maintain the drudgery, but also perfect the surveillance of the people. The private sphere will be yet more open to intrusion and inspection.

Hope is also a silent form of resistance. But for even the most optimistic, it must have worn thin; and many must have abandoned it altogether. It is very significant that the few voices openly raised in criticism have looked abroad for salvation.[54] The kind of radical internal reform required to prevent the situation from worsening is already too urgent to await the slow decay from within which autonomous local groups, often operating in ignorance of each other, as well as in fear of the secret police and its informers, can hope to achieve.

IV. Foreign Policy Gambits

Living on an Illusion

"The complications which may ensue in the East defy all calculation... But over there, beyond our frontiers, three or four hundred thousand individuals hanged, impaled, or with their throats cut, hardly count" – Metternich

Ceausescu's precise gifts as a politician in the domestic sphere are difficult to illustrate. Clearly, his consolidation of power in the cut-throat atmosphere of internal party strife required skill and timing of the highest order. But information about these events is fragmentary, self-contradictory and often misleading. By contrast, Ceausescu's virtuosity on the international scene has been played out in full public view, or at least with great publicity. It is now clear that the applause which he has often won from his Western admirers has recognised only the superficial features of his performance. His flattery of Western statesmen, and his attention to every detail of their comfort during their visits, were simply surface glitter, concealing duplicity and cynicism of an unusual intensity. Having scrambled to the top of their domestic greasy poles, Western politicians tend to forget that other people have had to rise by an altogether riskier route, where the stakes are much higher; and that their own democratic intrigues are child's play to someone who is accustomed to a game without any rules at all. As a result, they forget the first rule of card-sharps – never assume that you are the only player cheating.

Success in foreign policy, and the prestige which it confers, have been of immense importance to Ceausescu. Romanian propaganda remorselessly proclaims every meeting held between the *Conducator* and foreign leaders, with pride of place being given to evidence of his acceptance by Western statesmen as a valued partner, even as a friend. Combined with his occasional "snubs" to the Soviet Union, these contacts have undoubtedly helped to reinforce his domestic power-base.[55]

From the beginning of his period in office, Ceausescu upheld Gheorghiu-Dej's policy of insisting on the internal autonomy of each communist state in deciding upon matters of development and sovereignty. In April 1964, the RCP issued its famous "statement" about the Sino-Soviet split, denying the Soviet Communist Party the "leading role" in the world communist movement: "It is up to every Marxist-Leninist party, it is a sovereign right of each state", it noted, "to elaborate, choose or change the forms and methods of socialist construction... No party has, or can have, a privileged place; nor can it impose its line and opinions on other parties." Later, Ceausescu made elliptical criticisms of the Soviet-led invasion of Czechoslovakia in 1968.[56]

Ceausescu certainly dislikes the idea of Soviet hegemony, and disdains any interference in the internal affairs of other communist states. But when the illusion was created in 1968 that he was a closet liberal like Alexander Dubcek, his orthodox domestic policies were justified by Western sympathisers on the grounds that Ceausescu could not risk provoking Brezhnev by liberalising internally. In fact, he was doing the opposite; but he was also playing up to Romanian nationalism – or rather, to the Westerners who looked favourably upon it because it must, by definition, displease the Soviet Union. The devotees of amateur Kremlinology delighted in every nuance of Ceausescu's discourses. When he raised his glass to

"Bukovina," for example – not just "southern Bukovina", which Stalin left to Romania when he took the northern part, along with Bessarabia, in 1940 – Ceausescu was probably playing up to anti-Soviet resentments among the Romanian people, who include refugees from the Soviet Union's Moldavian republic.[57]

But the appeal to nationalism is not enough. The repetition of such gestures, even if it provides academics with something to "analyse", does not bring food to the people. By the time that Ceausescu was proving his independence from the Soviet Union by sending a team to the Los Angeles Olympics, and thereby gaining the renewal of Romania's "most favoured nation" status with the United States, he was already pressing for closer economic ties with the Soviet Union.[58]

Like Mao, with whom he enjoyed highly cordial relations, Ceausescu was critical of the changes in the Soviet Union after 1956 – and of the Soviet leadership's departure from the true path laid down by Stalin. Today too, "deviationism" is one of the Romanian leader's prime concerns. Both Peking and Moscow are objects of criticism for their *internal* policies:

> "We must bear in mind the fact that there are deviations – theoretical as well as practical, rightist as well as leftist. Of course, all are equally dangerous. However, in my opinion, *it is the rightist deviations that are most dangerous now*, for they can greatly harm socialist construction."[59]

Any departure from a centrally planned economy towards notions of "market socialism" are anathema to Ceausescu. He rejects the idea that the individual should be permitted to spend his own money "on whatever, and however, it strikes his mind". As for freedom, "there is full freedom of initiative – in implementing the plan," Ceausescu has observed.[60]

In the spring of 1985, the *Conducator* made one of his few genuinely memorable remarks, when he dismissed the idea that the Romanian party should move with the wind of change coming from Moscow. "Although there are some of us who think in this way," he observed, "we are not a debating club."[61] At a press conference with Western journalists early in July 1988, the wag of the regime, Stefan Andrei, representing Romania at the Comecon summit in Prague, expressed all the contempt and loathing of his boss for the idea of *glasnost* when he turned to his interpreter, saying that he did not understand the word and needed a translation.[62] Ceausescu's reorientation of Romania's trade towards the Soviet bloc over the last few years has, as a result, put him in an awkward, contradictory position, given his distaste for anything smacking of economic reform *à la russe*.

Ceausescu has been anxious to use the great power rivalry between China and the Soviet Union, as well as the divisions between the United States and the Soviet Union, to extend his own freedom of manoeuvre. His ideological conformity, at least until 1985, compensated the Kremlin for his uncomradely comments; but Romania lacks the strategic importance of Czechoslovakia, and is far less vulnerable to Western interference. Not even Ceausescu's flirting with the Chinese went very far. Instead, his cultivation of a harmonious relationship with the West, which enabled him to avoid becoming embroiled in the disturbances between the two blocs over Czechoslovakia, the Middle East and Afghanistan, was to the advantage of the Soviet Union in several ways. First, Romania acted as a conduit of diplomatic information and informal contacts, as it did with China. The greater willingness of Western states to sell high technology goods to Romania, and to permit Romanian inspectors and other personnel into their plants, provided the Soviet Union with valuable intelligence and economic advantages. Perhaps Ceausescu does not share everything with Moscow, or even as much as Moscow would like; but much of what he has been able to provide was probably unavailable to the Soviet Union from any other source. It is better for the Kremlin to get 70 per cent of Ceausescu's total than nothing at all.[63]

Third World Ventures

Although Ceausescu was anxious to dissociate Romania from the Soviet invasion of Afghanistan, in order to maintain its status as "most favoured nation", he had had no objections to Soviet and Cuban interventions in Africa – in support of "national liberation movements" and against domestic reactionaries – earlier in the decade. There were reasons much closer to the bone for his dislike of Brezhnev's decision. What alarmed Ceausescu and led him to criticise the invasion was similar to what had provoked Kim Il-Sung of North Korea. For the Red Army's initial action in December 1979 was not intended to deal with "counter-revolutionaries", but rather to settle the struggle for power between two quarrelling factions of the Afghan Communist Party. Neither Ceausescu nor Kim Il-Sung can have enjoyed watching the Soviet Union settle the succession issue in another socialist state.[64] The Vietnamese invasion of "Democratic Kampuchea", which for the moment disposed of Ceausescu's Khmer Rouge allies, was another uncomfortable precedent.

Nine years later, Ceausescu has felt confident enough to return to the issue, now that Moscow has all but admitted Brezhnev's mistake. At the end of April 1988, Ceausescu devoted a large part of his "exposé" to the Politburo to a discussion of international questions, and could not resist reiterating his criticism of both the Soviet Union and Vietnam for their respective interventions. A throw-away criticism of US support for the *Contras* in Nicaragua was probably less of a sop to Soviet feelings than another pin prick:

> "These conflicts have been strong arguments for the justness of the Marxist thesis against the export of revolution *and* counter-revolution. In effect, the Soviet troops... hardly helped Afghanistan on the path of socialism; on the contrary, they stimulated the growth of the counter-revolutionary forces, which led to the situation today. Nor were the Vietnamese troops of help in Kampuchea, where they brought damage and hardship."[65]

This did not mean that Ceausescu was renouncing the provision of indirect military assistance to national liberation movements. What he was demanding was an end to *military* intervention in internal affairs:

> "However, I must say that this does not mean renunciation of solidarity with the progressive anti-imperialist forces... We supported *and will continue to support* the peoples fighting for national independence... This is an essential line of our international policy of solidarity with all the anti-imperialist forces."[66]

It was hardly surprising, therefore, that the chairman of the Palestine Liberation Organisation, Yasser Arafat, had two days of talks with Ceausescu on 29–30 June 1988, which passed in a "cordial atmosphere of warm friendship...and mutual understanding."[67] But by maintaining diplomatic relations with Israel since 1967, Ceausescu has also provided himself with a fig-leaf of respectability – at least, as an armchair exponent of *realpolitik*. He regularly receives Israeli politicians; and there is, no doubt, some benefit to Israel too in holding discussions with a leader maintaining close relations with its sworn enemies. There is, however, another murkier aspect of relations between the only functioning democracy in the Middle East and Romania. Leaving aside the economic advantages to Romania, and the benefits to Israel which are likely to result from the deal with the Soviet Union to route future Soviet Jewish emigrants via Bucharest rather than Vienna (where too many have shown a tendency to regard the United States as their Promised Land), much of the business between the two countries is probably as lucrative as it is secret. Rumours abound of nuclear co-operation between Romania and Israel. Israel has provided the Romanian army with spare parts (presumably captured from the Arabs) for its tanks, and some design improvements. Israeli experience may also have helped with the designing of the new Romanian navy.[68]

Ceausescu also hoped to exercise an influence in the Third World as an arms supplier. In the early 1980s, he had some success; but more recently, the technical backwardness of Romanian weapons, and the likelihood of their poor performance even by this backward standard, has set back his ranking as a "merchant of death." Needless to say, the efforts to supply weapons were accompanied by a propaganda barrage in favour of disarmament. In the last few years, Romania has been spending proportionately less and less of its official budget on military forces and equipment. Its economic difficulties, and the use of the army for industrial work, help to explain this – even if, as is typical for the regime, spending on the least valuable arm, the navy, appears to have increased.[69]

A drive for autarky has been the distinctive feature of the economic policy of Romania throughout the period from Gheorghiu-Dej to Ceausescu. Although Ceausescu's diplomacy was slick and successful for almost two decades, however, the economic costs of becoming an "all-round multilaterally developed socialist society" have become obvious. These costs have been imposed by the unrealistic goals set by the leadership. Hoxha's Albania was able to preserve its independence by accepting the consequences of extreme isolation. Albanian "modernisation" has been slow; but the population appears to be better fed than that of Romania. By contrast, Ceausescu has been impatient. Like Gierek, he cut corners to get ahead. But he did not fall from power in the process; and he continues, as a result, to inflict enormous damage. He has turned Romania into an "under-developing country". But he has also tried, not surprisingly, to steal Tito's mantle as leader of the Third World.[70]

In the Economic Embrace

Ironically, Ceausescu's efforts to isolate Romania from the outside world have merely trapped it more firmly in the vice of unwelcome economic relations with the two Super Powers. In the 1970s, he borrowed willingly from the West to build up his industry. But the debt crisis of the early 1980s found Romania unable to fund its interest repayments with industrial goods. Ceausescu's planning mechanism seems to have pursued galloping obsolescence as an industrial ideal. Despite the fact that the Reagan Administration had proved no more anxious than its predecessor to take a firm line with Romania, Ceausescu decided to pay off his hard currency debts as rapidly as possible. This has required dumping on a massive scale.[71]

The West can be very capricious about the despots which it favours. But it should be noted that it was Ceausescu himself who gave notice to the bankers – as he did to the US Deputy Secretary of State, Arthur Whitehead, over "most favoured nation" status in February 1988. Realising that, in the Third World, the best guarantee of repayment lies not in the natural resources and economic order of a state, but in the efficiency of its state security system, the Western banks were still willing to lend to Romania. Yet since the early 1980s, Romania's trade has been reorientated increasingly towards Comecon and the least developed countries.[72]

Both Gheorghiu-Dej and Ceausescu resisted Soviet efforts to integrate the economies and planning systems of the Comecon states. Romania itself succeeded in remaining outside many of the mechanisms for common planning; and more recently, Bucharest has taken the lead in resisting the Gorbachev-Ryzhkov package of proposals, which would have the effect of integrating the Comecon economies on a bloc-wide level. This may reflect an ideological distaste for the market mechanisms which the Soviet Union wishes to introduce, as part of the process by which it hopes to make the group competitive in the world market. It may also reflect a fear over the possible loss of state sovereignty. Other states, like the German Democratic Republic and Bulgaria, have benefited from the existing arrangements and may not be anxious for change. Their objections to Moscow's plans are probably more straightforward. As the Bulgarian party leader, Todor Zhivkov, reputedly told the British Foreign Secretary, Sir Geoffrey Howe, in February 1985, economic success depends upon the possession of colonies: "Our first colony is the Soviet Union. It gives us raw materials like your colonies gave you, and we sell it back manufactured goods and exploit it as a market for our exports."[73]

Romania rejected similar opportunities whenever they arose; but now it finds itself in need of Soviet products – not least of petroleum, which it must pay for at the market price, even when bartering. Perhaps recognising the inevitability of the eventual withdrawal of "most favoured nation" status, because of his domestic repression, and aware also of the difficulty of off-loading Romanian manufactures on the West, Ceausescu took the decision to foster ever closer bilateral links with the Soviet Union. Perhaps he thought that he would still retain more autonomy that way. He may also have miscalculated the outcome of the Kremlin succession struggle.[74] For the moment, the Soviet Union is unlikely to use its rapidly growing economic ties with Romania to place pressure on Ceausescu to "liberalise". So long as he can perform his side of the bargain, that will suffice. But it may not always be so. He stretched Soviet patience by resisting the reform of Comecon in Prague – although on that occasion, as at the Vienna review meeting of the Conference on Security and Co-operation in Europe, Romania's obduracy had the secret sympathy of other East European states, who were happy to let Ceausescu take the blame.[75]

Indeed, the figures for the development of Romanian-Soviet trade must give the leadership in Bucharest pause for thought. It may be a much more difficult trend to reverse than that of economic links with the West. It is often just as expensive too, as oil imports have shown.[76] Romania's rapid expansion in energy consumption has outstripped its domestic fuel supplies. Earlier, its possession of 80 per cent of Comecon's non-Soviet oil production, and of substantial coal and natural gas resources, had encouraged Romanian independence. By 1973, the deliberate orientation of trade away from the Comecon countries had reduced the Soviet share of Romanian trade to about one-fifth, and the Comecon total to less than a half. But the fall of the Shah, and all that it brought in its train, created the conditions for a sudden turnaround. Trade with the West was savagely cut, particularly in the form of imports. The population has had to bear the burden of a policy which denies the necessity of importing anything which might conceivably be produced in the country (even when it is not), and which aims to export anything which can be sold abroad, at whatever price. Today, about 60 per cent of Romania's trade is with the Comecon countries. The Soviet Union takes more than one-third. A full 69 per cent of the food exported from Romania now also goes to the Soviet Union, including 24 per cent of all its meat. This is despite the Romanian government's claims that domestic hardships are being caused by grasping Western bankers.[77]

Although joint ventures and bilateral links might seem best suited to preserving Romanian autonomy, the development of co-production with the Soviet Union has also been very rapid – particularly in the last four years. It is intended that trade turnover should increase by 70 per cent in the period 1986–90. This has implications for security: not only is Romanian industry intertwined with its Soviet counterpart, but more and more Soviet "specialists" are also operating inside Romania.[78]

For the moment, however, Moscow is conferring medals rather than exerting pressure on Ceausescu. He himself recognizes that Gorbachev can hardly withdraw from Afghanistan, in the hope of mending fences with China, and then intervene in Romania. Why should he? Romania is doing its best to make *perestroika* a popular success by increasing the availability of meat and vegetables in the Soviet Union. Whether Ceausescu will be able to extricate himself, should the Soviet embrace become insistent in the future, remains to be seen. But he is probably not expecting Gorbachev's reforms to succeed any more readily than his own.[79]

Angry Neighbours

Ceausescu has no great problems with two immediate neighbours, Yugoslavia and Bulgaria. The Bulgarians object to the pollution of their atmosphere by Romanian industrial waste; but they can only regard the situation inside Romania with quiet satisfaction. Zhivkov himself shows little real enthusiasm for reform, although the quiet life seems to attract him in his declining years rather more than it attracts Ceausescu. Some Yugoslav newspapers have made noises about the impending fate of the Serbian minority in Romania; and Romanian refugees have tried to swim across the River Danube to Yugoslav territory. But a country of minorities, like Yugoslavia, cannot afford to raise the difficult question of the Serbs in Romania for fear of what might happen at home.[80]

The Hungarian government, however, has shown no such inhibitions. In the early summer of 1988, under pressure from his own population, and flushed with his assumption of the post of party General Secretary, the Hungarian ruler, Karoly Grosz, mixed bellicosity with sweet reason to ask and assure readers of the British *Financial Times*: "Should we have sharp words or troop concentrations, who would profit? No one."[81] But at the end of June, popular feeling and government frustration combined to permit the largest demonstration seen in Budapest since 1956, when tens of thousands of Hungarians, including some of the 25,000 refugees from Transylvania, protested against the forthcoming "systematisation" in front of the Romanian embassy. The event was greeted with fury by Ceausescu.

Just how far the Budapest demonstration was welcome to the new Hungarian regime cannot easily be ascertained. Clearly, Ceausescu himself did not believe that it could be "spontaneous" – Hungary is, after all, a communist country. But Hungary has also been the least brotherly, in its acceptance of so many refugees. The exchange of letters between the two parties, announced on 22 June, made clear their irreconcilable differences. The RCP accused the Hungarians of deliberately misrepresenting its policy. The Hungarian party replied that it attached "an immutable importance to the general situation of the Hungarian minority" in Romania.[82] So Ceausescu responded by closing the Hungarian consulate in Cluj. At the beginning of July, he addressed both the RCP Central Committee and the national council of the Socialist Democracy and Unity Front in provocative and insulting terms, threatening a complete breach in relations with Hungary. Without mentioning directly the existence of any minority in Romania, he accused the Hungarians of trying to "distract" attention from their own problems by playing up to "chauvinist, nationalist circles". In his vocabulary, this qualified them as "fascists", because they were "surpassing – and I say this with full responsibility – what even the 'Horthyists' dared to do." He told the Central Committee that the demonstrations were "organised with the agreement and – according to certain information from Hungary – under the patronage of, the official party and state bodies;" and he offered an assurance to the Front council:

> "We cannot accept the declaration of... the Hungarian parliament... that all citizens of other countries who have ancestors, however far removed, of Hungarian origin, are part of the Hungarian nation, and that Hungary takes responsibility to look after them... This is a concept alien to international law, which even Horthy did not dare to formulate."[83]

Ceausescu knows that a war between Romania and Hungary over Transylvania is not possible without Soviet approval. Furthermore, his alliance with Yugoslavia, which also has a Magyar minority, makes an attack by Hungary still less likely, even in the event of disorder in the Hungarian districts of Romania. Whether his excoriation of the Hungarian government, and of its attempts to revive the spectre of "revanchism" on the model of the 1940 Vienna Award, will rally popular support at home remains open to doubt. The Romanian-speaking majority would resent any external interference which was specifically designed to benefit the minorities; but whether they feel any enthusiasm for Ceausescu's vision is a very different question.

Grosz's own treatment at the hands of Ceausescu in August 1988 illustrates the *Conducator's* self-confidence. Having ignored Grosz's repeated suggestions of a summit meeting to discuss the effect of systematisation on the Hungarians in Transylvania, Ceausescu peremptorily summoned his Hungarian counterpart on a Thursday to meet the following Sunday at the border town of Arad.[84] The Hungarian spokesman quoted Soviet sources to the effect that the Soviet Union wanted to see an end to the "disruption" of relations, thereby implying criticism of both Hungary and Romania. But it was Grosz who had to come running when Ceausescu called. Ceausescu added humiliation to injury, furthermore, by permitting Grosz to give the impression to his own people and the world's press that "Arad opens a new chapter", before allowing the Romanian news agency, *Scinteia*, to renew its insults by accusing the Hungarians of interfering in internal Romanian affairs and denouncing the Hungarian party daily, *Nepszabadsag*, for echoing "hostile, chauvinistic and nationalistic circles and groups." Somewhat ludicrously, Romanians were reminded of Hungary's economic problems: "inflation.... marked unemployment, lack of housing and the like."[85]

Despite his abuse of the Hungarians for their concern about the survival of the culture of the Szeklers and other Magyars in Transylvania – as, indeed, about their physical well-being – Ceausescu has for long made a point of insisting on the duty of Romanians abroad to serve their "motherland", however distant their connections with it might be. It is, perhaps, precisely because of his own ambitions to build up a fifth column among Romanian *émigrés* that he is particularly sensitive to, and obstructive of, the efforts of Hungary and West Germany to foster the identity of the Hungarian and German-speaking minorities in Romania.[86] The West German government's policy of buying out the Germans who wish to leave has certain humanitarian merits, not least in today's climate. Unfortunately, however, the policy has also had the effect of isolating other minorities which do not have a wealthy patron. Furthermore, the desire to maintain the flow of emigrants has led Bonn to take a soft line with Romania on virtually everything, from credits to human rights. This has certainly exacerbated the internal disasters now afflicting all ethnic groups inside Romania. But it is now too late to reverse the policy, with an insistence on the strict recognition of minority rights. No one would wish to make martyrs of the Saxons and Swabians of the Banat, in a grand gesture against the decade of appeasement engineered by the West German Foreign Minister, Hans-Dietrich Genscher.

What is most striking about Ceausescu's foreign policy, as about all his policies, is how far he has been allowed to make the running. To be sure, there have been occasional benefits for the West. He facilitated the Nixon Administration's opening to Peking; but he enjoyed the gratitude of the United States long after he had ceased to play any useful role. Even as his own policies plunged Romania ever deeper into economic misery, both the International Monetary Fund and private Western banks, encouraged by Western governments, continued to help Ceausescu with the same policies as he moved further down the road to ruin. Instead of urging a return to real domestic self-sufficiency, they were prepared to fund yet more prestige projects, which would destroy the infrastructure of the country and make debt repayments less likely. This was as true, furthermore, of the Reagan Administration as it was of its predecessors. The US Secretary of State, George Schultz, proved no more realistic about Ceausescu's motivations and interests than General Alexander Haig, who seems to have believed that "playing ball with the bad guys" was proof of a commendable understanding of *realpolitik*.[87] Instead, it was pressure from outside the magic circle of diplomatic experts which first began to unravel the Romanian connection. Ceausescu's obduracy had begun to frustrate Western purposes more than Soviet aims. Suddenly he had become a villain – a villain with a trade surplus.

Ceausescu's diplomatic alchemy may now be wearing thin; but he is still enjoying certain advantages from it, particularly at an internal level. At the Warsaw Pact's Warsaw summit in July 1988, he replied on behalf of his colleagues – who included Karoly Grosz – to the toast of General Wojciech Jaruzelski, the Polish leader; and the Romanian media presented this as evidence of Ceausescu's influential role, even though it was no more than a matter of protocol. His visits to ever more obscure Third World states have also helped to preserve his standing as a "world statesman". He has friends, bound by common interest, in China and Yugoslavia; and whilst his only real enemy, Hungary, is impotent to act unilaterally against him, he can also feel confident that the Soviet Union will refrain from taking action. As for the West, Romania still remains a far-away country, about which the less said the better.

V. Conclusion: Some Western Responses

Prediction is a thankless task. What is likely to happen in Romania, and between Romania, its neighbours and the rest of the world, is so dependent on contingent and unforeseeable events that any would-be prognosticator is almost certain to come unstuck, even in the short term. It can be stated confidently, however, that Nicolae Ceausescu will remain both arbitrary in his methods and obstinate in his pursuit of goals, thus rendering internal reform improbable until he is removed by death or physical incapacity from power. Despite frequent rumours of ill health, Ceausescu's recent public appearances do not suggest that his demise is imminent.[88] Men in their seventies sometimes drop dead; but "great helmsmen" all too often display an unpalatably dogged longevity. Only a few more years of Ceausescu's policies will make comparisons between Romania and Ethiopia, and between Ceausescu and Pol Pot, still more credible.

Relations between Ceausescu's regime and the Soviet Union may not be good; but Moscow's leverage over Romania is limited. As noted above, Romanian trade has been reorientated increasingly in the last eight years towards the socialist bloc. But whether Gorbachev will use Romania's increasing dependence upon the Soviet Union, for such commodities as fuel, to modify Ceausescu's internal policies remains to be seen. So far, he has shown no overt interest in doing so. Since the Soviet Communist Party does not remotely possess the residual authority over RCP appointments which Brezhnev asserted against the Czechoslovak leader, Alexander Dubcek, in 1968, or which it still seems to possess in relation to other Warsaw Pact states, it is difficult to see how Gorbachev could engineer a palace coup, even if he wished to do so. Ceausescu, for his part, has gone to great lengths to root out potential supporters of a "Moscow orientation" within the party and secret police apparatus.[89]

In foreign affairs, there may be no advantage for the Soviet Union in making Romania tow Moscow's line any more than at present. Rather, the main benefit for the Soviet Union lies in preserving Ceausescu's "maverick" stance – even though its own credibility in the West is waning fast. During Gorbachev's first two years as General Secretary of the CPSU, several intellectuals expressed the hope that he might try to influence events in Romania, since he represented "technocratic-orientated and rational approaches to policy".[90] When Gorbachev visited Bucharest in May 1987, he alluded to the need to remove corrupt and nepotic cadres – in a speech containing specific references to his policies in the Soviet Union, but which was not lost on his Romanian audience. On the other hand, he also emphasised – as he did in Yugoslavia in March 1988 – that the socialist countries should enjoy "total independence in the definition of their political line." A similar acknowledgement – counterbalancing, to a large extent, the implicit criticisms – was made by Gorbachev during Ceausescu's visit to Moscow in early October 1988.[91]

The apparently intractable dispute between the republics of Armenia and Azerbaijan over the region of Nagorno-Karabakh has also lessened the likelihood that the current Soviet leadership will put pressure on Bucharest to retreat from the policy of "systematisation", despite all its implications for Hungarian-Romanian relations. As nationality problems become more acute in the Soviet Union – and in other socialist states, especially Yugoslavia – Romania's own minorities will probably be left to stew by Gorbachev, along with the rest of the population. So far, the *Pax Sovietica* has kept the nationalities problem in Eastern Europe under a modicum of control; but it is as far from a solution as ever. With agitation for at least greater autonomy growing amongst minorities within the Soviet Union itself, Gorbachev is hardly likely to complicate the situation even further by embarking on a quixotic crusade on behalf of the peasantry of Transylvania. Evidently, his rhetoric about "our common European house" does not extend to an active concern about what is going on next-door. When its own interests are at stake, the Soviet leadership will evidently turn a blind eye to cultural genocide, and to much more besides.

The Kremlin must be well aware of how shortlived any Western applause for intervention in Romania would be. Ceausescu has learnt about the fickleness of the West himself: without any alteration in his methods, his rating has moved from friend and hero, to monster and tyrant. As its planned withdrawal from Afghanistan and its apparent pressure on Vietnam over the occupation of Kampuchea have shown, the Soviet Union is anxious to mend its fences with China; and the latter's hostility to overt intervention in Romania or indirect pressure on Ceausescu would be intense. Yugoslavia would be in a still more difficult position, given its defensive alliance with Romania.

The Soviet Union appears to have encouraged the Hungarian government to cool tempers as far as possible.[92] It does not want the Balkan hornets' nest to be stirred up. So long as order reigns in Bucharest and the "socialist system" in Romania is not threatened, therefore, matters should be left alone. But the stability of Karoly Grosz's regime is probably more at risk than that of Ceausescu over the "systematisation" of the Hungarian villages in Transylvania. It is, indeed, in a peculiarly awkward position. If it protests too vigorously against Ceausescu's plans, then it will raise the spectre of revanchism, which will worry its other neighbours, who also have Magyar minorities – Czechoslovakia, Yugoslavia and, above all, the Soviet Union. But if it remains silent, it risks becoming discredited in the eyes of its own people. Any visitor to Hungary who has raised the subject can testify to the passions which the impending demolitions arouse. The fact that sympathy is often expressed for the Romanian people as well does not diminish the necessity for Grosz's regime to avoid antagonising such profound national sentiment. In these circumstances, Moscow can only hope that Grosz will find an *internal* solution.

To a great extent, despite his differences with the Soviet Union and Hungary, Ceausescu has reason to be satisfied with his relations with the communist world. At present, its internal contradictions are working to his benefit; and his own repressive regime faces a less acute challenge to its authority than his more tolerant and hated Hungarian neighbour. The downward spiral of Romanian society is unlikely to be hindered, let alone stopped, by forces from within the country, or from the Soviet bloc. The viability of his "Albanian option" remains open.

If Romania's own neighbours and allies are neither able nor willing to influence its internal politics, it is difficult to think of measures which might be taken by the West to improve the situation. But it would be a mistake, nonetheless, to conclude that, given the Ceausescu regime's façade of immobility and bloody-mindedness, any Western action must necessarily prove ineffective. Clearly, no single Western government can expect to exercise a decisive influence: unilateral actions by the British government, for instance, where they have any tangible consequences, will be easily circumvented. But collective action by Western states, and particularly by the West European states, might produce positive results.

Here is an opportunity for the European Economic Community to show that it is more than an inward-looking cartel. Despite its declining share of Romanian trade, the developed West still accounts for an appreciable proportion – over one-fifth of the total. Since this trade is based on the willingness of Western states to accept dumping, furthermore, no free trader would need to object if restrictions were placed upon it. At present, much of what is exported to the West is sold at below cost price. On 16 August 1987, Karoly Kiraly, who had been the last influential ethnic Hungarian in the RCP hierarchy, wrote to Ceausescu demanding the answer to a pressing question:

> "How is it possible to ignore man and his needs with such callousness?... The last loaf of bread is being exported out of the people's mouth; and goods are being exported systematically for below production costs, riding roughshod over the needs of those who sweat to produce these goods."[93]

Mihai Botez, a mathematician and former planning strategy adviser to the Romanian government, has criticised the Western states for permitting and, indeed, encouraging the impoverishment and degradation of his country:

> "Instead of promoting an economy which works, or socialism with a human face, you have helped to legitimise a corrupt communist regime, which has ruined our country."[94]

Of course, the grant of "most favoured nation" status to Romania by the United States has now come to an end, thereby lessening American connivance at the export of vital foodstuffs. But other states should be discouraged from taking up the slack. In contrast with the imposition of economic sanctions against South Africa – which must, at least initially, hurt those whom they are intended to help – the refusal to purchase food exports from Romania cannot hurt the Romanian people. Even if Ceausescu were bloody-minded (or incompetent) enough to let the food rot, rather than distribute it within the country, the loss of hard currency earnings would, at least, hinder some of his other projects, which threaten the happiness, and even the lives, of his subjects.

Similarly, sanctions against non-food exports would not necessarily harm the Romanian population, whilst the refusal to export goods or credits would have only a minute effect on employment in the boycotting countries themselves. The net result might even be a positive one, if dumped Romanian products were refused entry. The few Western businessmen who profit from the sweating labour of Romanians, and from the distorted market thus created, would no doubt protest against this inferference with "free trade"; but it is difficult to imagine that such a situation would be tolerated against a background of similar oppression and hardship elsewhere. Even Sweden's economy would survive, if an unusually moral stance were adopted with a refusal to export any more bulldozers and earth-moving equipment to Romania. Perhaps the Slavery Society, whose predecessors in the late 1920s and early 1930s tried to alert the West to Stalin's use of slave labour to provide competitive exports, could also turn the spotlight on Romania.

If a variety of economic sanctions would hinder, if not halt, Ceausescu's destructive mania, however the West should avoid a blanket boycott of Romania as a whole. Intellectual and personal contacts with Romanians outside the regime should be encouraged – to hold a normal conversation with someone who is not an informer is of inestimable value. But all official contacts, beyond the barest minimum required for diplomatic relations, should be avoided – the breaking of diplomatic relations would merely isolate internal campaigners for human rights. Western diplomats should, however, be encouraged, in recognition of the cavalier practices of Romanian officials, to use diplomatic contacts, wherever possible, as conduits for passing information and materials to a wider public. Naturally, conditions under such a regime make it difficult to do anything very effective. But at the moment, with few if any exceptions, the Western diplomatic community is not generally considered to have exerted even limited muscle-power, to the minimal degree already tolerated by the Romanian regime. This is a disgraceful blot on their honour and their professionalism. Only the West Germans have some excuse to avoid upsetting the *Conducator*; and even then, the existence of 200,000 "hostages" is a justification for caution, not for the indifference which Romanians detect. For too long, Western diplomats and cultural representatives have viewed their task as being to represent Ceausescu's views and justifications to their own governments, rather than to promote the interests and values of their own countries.

It is a paradox that, although the regime preaches autarky and discourages contacts with foreigners on the part of its own subjects, Ceausescu's travels abroad and international visitors at home are constantly publicised in a bid to give legitimacy to his rule. A concerted effort to withdraw such "photo-opportunities" by the representatives of democratic states, beginning with those of the European Community, might be little more than a pin-prick; but to such a sensitive potentate, prolonged exclusion would prove unusually damaging.

An opportunity for Western politicians to express their contempt for Ceausescu's rule, albeit at the expense a free trip with "perks" to his "Golden Age", is coming soon. The Seventh Inter-Parliamentary Conference is due to be held in Bucharest in 1989. Romanian propaganda proclaims that the choice of this least parliamentary of capitals as the site for a meeting which will also mark the centenary of the Inter-Parliamentary Union, "[has] tellingly confirmed... the importance of the dynamic activity of Romania... [and] the appreciation and prestige enjoyed worldwide by the theoretical and practical work of President Nicolac Ccausescu."[95] By refusing to participate in this grotesque jamboree, the British members of the Inter-Parliamentary Union can at least do something to compensate the Romanian public for the unwitting connivance shown by a delegation of five British Members of Parliament on a visit to the country in July 1988, whose ignorance and complacency caused astonishment and deep offence to ordinary Romanians.[96]

Another way of undermining the prestige of Ceausescu – and, not least, of restoring the honour of the West – would be for Western states and institutions which have bestowed titles and other distinctions on Ceausescu and his wife to withdraw them. At the same time, they should also refuse or return any honours offered or granted to them by the Romanian regime or its institutions. When Ceausescu paid his state visit to Britain in 1978, for instance, the Queen herself decorated him with the insignia and rank of a "Knight Grand Cross of the Most Honourable Order of the Bath". Whatever the illusions suffered by her humble advisers then, it is hardly appropriate that such a man should retain this honour today. The Queen should be advised to withdraw the honour, and to return the Star of the Socialist Republic of Romania which she received in turn. This can hardly be among her most treasured mementoes.

Such a course of action might, in turn, give a lead to Britain's Royal Institution of Chemists to expel Elena Ceausescu, "the world-ranking scientist and academician," from its list of honorary members. Perhaps the Central London Polytechnic could also strike a blow for academic freedom by withdrawing her honorary doctorate.

There must be other institutions in Britain, in addition to similarly august bodies abroad, which have such Romanian skeletons in their cupboards. In most cases, such niceties date from a different era, in which wishful thinking about Ceausescu's "resolute independence" from Moscow, and paternalistic concern for his country, ran deep. With no sign of any incipient change of policy towards Romania on the part of the British and other Western governments, furthermore, it is hardly surprising that the honours and decorations should have remained in place. But it is remarkable that, until now, no overt pressure should have been exerted for their withdrawal by non-governmental organisations, churches and other bodies. The corrosive effect of the regime's public repudiation would be considerable, particularly if it could be communicated to the Romanian people themselves. Perhaps the National Museum in Bucharest would even feel obliged to withdraw such decorations from display in the salons devoted to the "homage" paid to Ceausescu – where everything, from the ribbon of the *Légion d'Honneur* to a certificate of Honorary Citizenship of Disneyland, purportedly testifies to his acceptance abroad.

Since sport is nationalised in Romania – as it is throughout the communist world – and promoted for state purposes, a boycott of bilateral sporting events might also help to damage

Ceausescu's public standing, just as the participation of Romania in the 1984 Los Angeles Olympics, and in other competitions with Western teams, helped to bolster it. Unfortunately, the sportsmen and sporting organisers of Britain are more likely to regard socialist Romania's methods of producing champions as being worthy of emulation than as reasons for disgust.[97]

Access to information is essential, not only for the creation of well-informed oppositional circles, who may be encouraged to have the confidence to promote rational alternatives as far as possible, but also, and in some ways more importantly now, to preserve the morale and sanity of those who must live cut off from the outside world. The Romanian service of the British Broadcasting Corporation enjoys a high reputation among Romanian listeners. But the Foreign and Commonwealth Office's approach to the funding of the service represents a classic Whitehall compromise: when there are increases, they come across the board; and when there are cuts, they fall on all services equally. At a time of crisis, even an extra hour each day would greatly help people who are often ignorant of events inside Romania, let alone of events in the world beyond. The FCO and its Parliamentary paymasters could do much for Britain's reputation in Eastern Europe as a whole by handling matters sensitively. At a time when opposition circles in other Soviet bloc countries are making a great effort to protest against Ceausescu's policies, additional help for the BBC's Romanian service would be widely welcomed.[98]

Direct material aid to Romania is effectively ruled out by the regime's refusal to accept "charity", on the grounds that it is unneeded and insulting.[99] But the Hungarian government has permitted humanitarian assistance from the West to reach the 25,000 refugees from Romania who have received asylum there. Western aid agencies and governments should be taking more notice of their plight.

As demonstrated above, relations with Ceausescu's Romania have hardly benefited the Western states at all. A few businessmen have done well out of the country's impoverishment, just as the Armand Hammers of 60 years ago did well out of the famine-stricken Soviet Union. But Romania's obdurate stand over such issues as the Helsinki process has revealed not only Ceausescu's contempt for human rights but also his willingness to block military and other forms of co-operation which are of "practical" interest to the West. Sudden displays of Western irritation should represent more than occasional releases of hot air. If the Western states make their disavowal of Ceausescu's regime complete, and give it the necessary publicity, it will be more difficult for his Warsaw Pact allies to treat their own visits to Romania as part of the normal routine. Next year, the regular summit of Warsaw Pact leaders is due to take place in Bucharest, possibly in the new Palace of the People. It will be an opportunity for the Western media and Western governments to state their positions clearly.

In the meantime, since dramatic internal changes are unlikely in the short term, and since Ceausescu's allies have their own concerns, co-ordinated measures should be taken by the Western states, as a matter of urgency, to isolate Ceausescu's regime and assist his subjects. Such measures offer the only remaining hope of delaying or curbing his plans to desecrate his country's heritage and drive his population beyond the brink of despair. In Stalin's time, the unprecedented urge to create utopia, regardless of the cost, assumed practical form when ignorance of its consequences was still widespread, and when wishful thinking muddied many minds. Today, we can only deny the consequences of Ceausescu's polices by turning a blind eye.

Notes

1 *The Times*, 14 June 1978.

2 See Mervyn Stockwood, "The Big Improvements", in *The Times*, 12 June 1978.

3 Worrall's commentary was carried in "The World at One"; BBC Radio Four, 24 November 1987. For Sonnenfeldt's statement, see the *Frankfurter Allgemeine Zeitung*, 15 July 1988. The French, German and Italian press have given more serious and regular coverage to events in the Balkans than any of the British newspapers. British reporters trying to produce an accurate analysis, like Richard Bassett of *The Times* and Nicholas Thorpe of *The Independent*, have quickly found themselves being expelled and refused re-entry.

4 Ion Pacepa, *Red Horizons*; Heinemann, London, 1988. Although no mention is made of this, the text suggests the existence of a "ghost-writer" or assistant, as does the Romanian translation of the *English* original. Anyone inclined to doubt Pacepa's portrait of the paranoid Romanian elite should compare his account with the comments of the late Albanian dictator, Enver Hoxha, on the security precautions taken by the Romanian leadership; see Jon Halliday, ed., *The Artful Albanian: Memoirs of Enver Hoxha*; Chatto and Windus, London, 1986, pp. 123–4, 285. The Hungarian leader, Janos Kadar, was reputedly amazed by Ceausescu's employment of a food-taster; see Michael Shafir, *Romania: Politics, Economics and Society – Political Stagnation and Simulated Change*; Francis Pinter, London, 1985, p. 186.

5 David B. Funderburk, *Pinstripes and Reds: An American Ambassador Caught between the State Department and the Romanian Communists, 1981–1985*; Selous Press, Washington D.C., 1987, pp. 13ff.

6 The slogan is displayed prominently in "The Epoch of Nicolae Ceausescu", in *Revista saptaminalia editata de Frontul Democratiei si Unitatii Socialiste*, 16 July 1988.

7 Ilie Ceausescu, *Transylvania: An Ancient Romanian Land*; Military Publishing House, Bucharest, 1983, p. 3.

8 See, for example, "A Conscious Forgery of History under the Aegis of the Hungarian Academy of Sciences", in *The Times*, 7 April 1987; placed by "C. Marino, St. Meletiou 186, Athens". West German readers have also been given the opportunity to inform themselves of the official Romanian view of Transylvania's history, in a lavishly produced journal devoted to the subject; see the *Frankfurter Allgemeine Zeitung*, 6 July 1988. The offending Hungarian volume, *Erdely Története*, was published in Budapest in 1986, under the editorship of the Hungarian Minister of Culture, Béla Köpeczi. Despite firing the opening shot in this latest round of the dispute, the Hungarian government does not spend hard currency on publicising such cases in the West.

9 Quoted in Ceausescu, op. cit., p. 38.

10 Personal information supplied by local citizens and foreign diplomats in Bucharest. See also *NRC Handelsblad*, 6 August 1988; and *The Sunday Times*, 14 August 1988. Rumours of plans for passive resistance, and in some cases of active defiance, are widespread; but there is little evidence of any action. Surprise is important: the government knows where it will strike next, while the peasants have no warning. In certain districts, the local people failed to identify the likely targets, even when the bulldozers had moved into the area.

11 See Albert Speer, *Inside the Third Reich*; Collins, London, 1970. Speer describes the reasoning behind the wilful destruction of architectural monuments which had survived the Allied bombing: "Away with the castles and churches – after the war we'll build our own monuments! In part, this impulse sprang from a feeling of inferiority toward the past that the party big-wigs had. But there was another element in this feeling, as one of the *Gauleiters* explained when he was justifying his demolition order to me: castles and churches of the past were citadels of reaction that stood in the way of our revolution"; ibid., p. 429. A cover photograph, published by *Contemporanul* in February 1988, of Nicolae and Elena Ceausescu gazing across an architectural model, compares strikingly with the photographs of Hitler and his models. One of Ceausescu's secretaries is said to have described the family's penchant for playing with toy buildings; *NRC Handelsblad*, 6 August 1988.

12 *Libération*, 25 November 1987. See also Raymond Lark, "Bulldozing Bucharest", in *The Spectator*, 7 May 1988.

[13] See Strobe Talbot, ed., *Khrushchev Remembers*; Collins, London, 1971, p. 51ff; and Geoffrey Hosking, *A History of the Soviet Union*; Collins, London, 1985, pp. 437–43. See also Trotsky's *Literature and Revolution*; Moscow, 1924.

[14] On the Danube-Black Sea Canal, see Vlad Georgescu, "Romania in the 1980s: The Legacy of Dynastic Socialism", in *Eastern European Politics and Societies*, No. 1, 1988.

[15] For an analysis of the development of the Romanian navy, in the context of Romania's general economic needs, see Robert Van Tol and Jonathan Eyal, "The New Romanian Navy: A Weapon without a Target", in the *RUSI Journal*, March 1987. Romania has become one of the world's leading steel producers, importing enormous quantities of ore, but exporting less than 15 per cent of its finished steel in an already glutted world market; see the figures cited in Georgescu, op. cit.

[16] For the regulations introduced in January 1984, see Shafir, op cit., pp. 46–8.

[17] Georgescu, op. cit. Professor Oprea Parpala published a critique of the running of Romanian agriculture, citing examples of mismanagement bordering on the farcial, in *Revista Economica*, August 1985; see Paul Gafton, "Economic Malaise and Remedies", in Vojtech Mastny, ed., *An Annual Soviet-East European Survey, 1985–1986*; Durham, 1987, pp. 306–8.

[18] English text issued by Agerpress, 4 March 1988.

[19] From "Exposé on Questions of Socioeconomic Management, Ideological and Political-Educational Work, and the International Situation at the Meeting of the Executive Political Committee of the Central Committee of the Romanian Communist Party", in *Romania Today*, May 1988. For the relevant figures, see Sophia M. Miskiewicz and Aaron Trehub, "The Chronic Housing Deficit", in Mastny, op. cit., pp. 179–81.

[20] *Frankfurter Allgemeine Zeitung*, 22 June 1988.

[21] Quoted in *Romanian News*, 22 July 1988. For details of sanitary, plumbing and heating provisions in the new housing blocks, see Dan Ionescu, "Housing as a Political Tool", in *Radio Free Europe: Romanian Situation Report*, 6 November 1987.

[22] *Romanian News*, 22 July 1988. See the anonymous letter from "A Group of Intellectuals", in Miskiewicz and Trehub, op. cit., p. 180: "The life in blocks of apartments...means living under the close scrutiny of your neighbours. It represents a new way of life in which the behaviour and requirements of the collective body are present at every moment. It is a new social environment in which priority is given to the collectivity over the individual". Traditional Romanian rural architecture would only be "preserved in folk art museums".

[23] Agerpress, supra.

[24] See "Exposé on Questions", supra; and Viorel Oradeanu, "Stairway to Slatina", in *Romania Today*, May 1988. In this article, Ion Manea, the mayor of Slatina, shows the reporter an album of old photographs of his town, with the remark, "Until 1980, only a few blocks of flats were built; but from 1980 onwards, the entire town actually got new looks. Therefore, we preserve the pictures of the old town as elements of comparison". At the beginning of July 1988, the Party newspaper, *Scinteia*, reported on the "reconstruction" around Ilfov near Bucharest. It named two demolished villages of less than 3000 inhabitants, where the people had been moved to new centres: "The move was easier for the young people of the villages of Buda and Ordreanu than for the elderly...Although the people now live in civilised conditions in their new houses, it is difficult for them to give up the customary way of life which they pursued in the villages"; *Züricher Tages-Anzeiger*, 15 July 1988. Ceausescu himself supervised the start of the operation.

[25] *The Times*, 17 December 1987. Ceausescu did not specify which parts of a chicken would be available for domestic consumption. The United Nations has estimated that Romanians spend the highest proportion of their family budgets on food of any Comecon country; see Shafir, op. cit., p. 118.

[26] Many Romanians can tell horror stories about this. The lack of gas pressure in the autumn of 1987 also led to a breakdown in the crematoria, necessitating the use of mass graves; *The Sunday Telegraph*, 15 November 1987.

[27] For additional examples, see William Crowther, "Romanian Politics and the International Economy", in *Orbis*, Fall 1984.

[28] On the treatment of infants and the elderly, see the anonymous article, "Birth and Death in Romania", in *The New York Review of Books*, 23 October 1986. The tactic of registering births after one month is widely used, so that the infant mortality rate can be kept within respectable bounds. Ceausescu has also launched a "special programme" to support the moving of pensioners from big cities to the countryside, where they will be able to "develop a certain useful activity"; see Anneliite Gabanyi, "Romanian Pensioners Barred from Moving to Popu-

lation Centres", in *Survey*, Vol. 29, No. 4, August 1987. About 40,000 elderly people have been moved from Bucharest in this way.

[29] See, for example, Constanta Nita, "23 Million", in *Romania Today*, June 1988. The article celebrated the birth of Ceausescu's 23 millionth subject. *Romana Libera*, 8 February 1986, proclaimed that a pregnant woman is "everybody's concern" in socialist Romania, where family life is "a socialised private problem". Ceausescu announced, a few days later, that "a house with many children is proof of a good citizen's concern for the nation's future"; *Scinteia*, 11 February 1986.

[30] For the effects of Ceausescu's family planning and medical policies on the average Romanian family, see *Der Spiegel*, 28 December 1987.

[31] Dan Ionescu, "Abortion in Romania", in *Survey*, supra. Of course, the offering of inducements for illegal operations or for jumping the queue, and the demanding of them, are not unique to Romania. Abortion is the most common means of birth control in the Soviet Union too.

[32] Quoted in Lord Moran, *Winston Churchill: The Struggle for Survival, 1940–1965*; Thomas Nelson, London, 1966, p. 82.

[33] *Frankfurter Allgemeine Zeitung*, 4 December 1987. No opposition was offered by officials either in the party headquarters or in the People's Council building opposite; see *East European Reporter*, Vol. 3, No. 2, March 1988. There were reports that a senior police officer had been killed; *The Independent*, 27 November 1987. But this goes against the trend of eye-witness and second-hand accounts. A variety of "luxury" goods, including bananas and pineapples, were "liberated" during the demonstration; *The Independent*, 24 December 1987.

[34] *Frankfurter Allgemeine Zeitung*, 14 December 1987; and *The Times* (AP), 15 December 1987. By the end of April, Ceausescu was less inclined to make concessions: "Many of the problems in recent months…are the result of a lack of firmness…We must work resolutely to enhance responsibility, and to strengthen order and discipline in work, in all areas of activity…Our broad democratic system must in no way weaken or lessen order and discipline; on the contrary!…Lawfulness and revolutionary humanism demand a firm attitude against those people who disregard the general interests of socialist society"; see "Exposé on Questions", supra.

[35] *The Independent*, 28 November 1987.

[36] Ibid.

[37] Quoted in Georgescu, op. cit.

[38] Gorbachev's efforts to bring Brezhnev's provincial satraps to order in the Soviet Union are broadly analogous; and Silviu Brucan makes an explicit comparison. Referring to the decisions of the Nineteenth CPSU Conference of June 1988, he notes that "the idea of giving the party leader the additional post of president, with extraordinary executive powers over legislation…foreign policy, defence and so on", is "not an exception. The conference decided that the party leader at each level should be nominated automatically to head the local soviet… Romania is the only socialist country to have experienced such a merger in recent history. As a Romanian Marxist, I am amazed that reformers in Moscow should want to emulate that model"; see the *International Herald Tribune*, 6–7 August 1988.

[39] Khrushchev argued that Stalin had expanded the size of the Presidium as a means of enhancing his authority, and as the prelude to a purge; see Talbot, op. cit., pp. 246–9. The Central Committee has about 425 full and candidate members. The Politburo has about 40 members, with an inner core of 14 making up its standing committee. Ceausescu's wife, Elena, who has chaired the Commission on Cadres in Party and State since 1979, is also a member of the standing committee, controlling the *nomenklatura*. But it was suggested that, by 1985, Ceausescu's arbitrary personnel changes might have threatened his authority. For comparative figures, see Shafir, op. cit., pp. 75–6.

[40] See, for example, *The Daily Telegraph*, 15 December 1987. For additional details of the family network, see Vladimir Tismaneanu, "Byzantine Rites, Stalinist Follies", in *Orbis*, Spring 1986; and René de Flers, "Socialism in One Family", in *Survey*, Vol. 28, No. 4, Winter 1984. Ceausescu is not the only communist ruler to have surrounded himself with family members. Leaving aside his own "role-model", Kim Il-Sung of North Korea, the "Latin" communists, Fidel Castro and Daniel Ortega, have both placed their own brothers in charge of their respective Defence Ministries.

[41] The insecurity of a pensioned existence out of power has made Soviet bloc leaders unwilling to "retire"; and it is difficult to imagine the Ceausescu family being left to pass their remaining days picking mushrooms like Khrushchev. As one commentator has put it, "If Khrushchev was accused…of setting up a cabinet of friends and relatives, one wonders how the resolution of the Romanian Central Committee would read"; Shafir, op. cit., p. 94. But the *nomenklatura* of Romania is relatively minuscule. By its broadest definition, it consists of about

200,000 people, or less than one per cent of the population. By comparison, under the "second serfdom" at the beginning of the Nineteenth Century, the boyar class of Moldavia and Wallachia represented about two per cent of the population; and in Transylvania, the nobles formed a still higher proportion.

[42] Both Ceausescu and Jaruzelski have been heads of their respective Main Political Military Directorates. Ceausescu's brother, Ilie, is currently chairman of the Higher Political Council of the Romanian Armed Forces – as the Romanian directorate is now called – as well as being a deputy Defence Minister. For an analysis of the network system, see James Sherr, *Soviet Power: The Continuing Challenge*; Macmillan, London, 1987, pp. 77–8.

[43] See *Frankfurter Allgemeine Zeitung*, 25 March 1988.

[44] The silence of the Patriarchate during the demolition of parishes has been a classic indication of this acquiescent attitude. Another was its silence when at least 20,000 Bibles, sent to Romania by the World Reformed Alliance, were pulped to make toilet paper; see Vladimir Socor, "Mounting Religious Repression", in Mastny, op. cit., pp. 309–10. It is little wonder that the regime finds no need to accompany the physical destruction of churches with strident "scientific atheistic" propaganda, as Stalin and Khrushchev did when "liberating" the Soviet population from the thrall of "superstition".

[45] On officially sponsored anti-semitism, see Michael Shafir, "The Men of Archangel Revisited: Anti-Semitic Formations among Romania's Intellectuals", in *Studies in Comparative Communism*, No. 16, 1983. For two recent views on the controversial role of Romania's Chief Rabbi, see Jessica Douglas-Home, "Romania's Chief Rabbi dances to Ceausescu's tune", in *The Wall Street Journal*, 28 June 1988; and Charles Hoffman, "Romania's Miracle", in *The Jewish Chronicle*, 29 July 1988.

[46] See *Radio Free Europe: Romanian Situation Report*, 3 July 1987.

[47] For severe criticism of the Romanian intelligentsia's "passivity", see Shafir, op. cit., pp. 148–52. Several later oppositionists, like the exiled poet, Paul Goma, who cannot be accused of passivity, had earlier written or spoken in Ceausescu's honour.

[48] *The Independent*, 28 November 1987.

[49] The lack of enthusiasm and concern even extends to the *apparatchiki*. Ceausescu himself has detected the mood of stagnation: "I must say that I have the impression that there is a certain mentality with some activists – 'I will be criticised again, I will once again admit my mistakes, I will make some more pledges; and that will be all' "; see "Exposé on Questions", supra.

[50] Romania has had "multi-candidate" elections since the mid-1970s; but all candidates have to be approved by the SDUF, and constituencies represented by "distinguished personalities" never field more than one candidate. As with Gorbachev's proposed system in the Soviet Union, the party secretary at each level chairs the local Front unit, which selects the candidates. As in other communist states, casting a negative vote is a more convoluted process than casting a positive one. It also tends to attract attention to the voter, as does spoiling one's ballot, the result of which can be demotion, "re-location" or dismissal from work. The names of negative voters tend not to reappear on the revised electoral registers. But a negative or missing vote is embarrassing to the officials responsible.

[51] Ceausescu thrust all responsibility for the disaster on his subordinates. Seven officials were jailed; and the Minister of Foreign Trade, Ilie Vaduva, and Chairman of the State Planning Committee, Stefan Birlea, were sacked. Other ministers too, including the Premier, Constantin Dascalescu, were "criticised" by Ceausescu. The official admission of "mistakes" is so rare that many locals are left terrified at the thought of what the truth must have been. See *The Times*, 20 July 1988, and *Le Monde*, 19–20 June 1988.

[52] The Romanian Democratic Action report appears to have been the first independent attempt to survey the effects of the haphazard disposal of waste, toxic matter and infected human material over 40 years; see *Radio Free Europe: Romanian Situation Report*, 2 March 1988; and *Frankfurter Allgemeine Zeitung*, 30 July 1988.

[53] *Romania Today*, June 1988.

[54] As in the case of Brucan, who believed that "the prevailing trend in the East" should persuade Ceausescu to respond to the Brasov events with reform rather than repression; *The Independent*, 28 November 1987.

[55] The US Deputy Assistant Secretary of State, Thomas Simons, for example, remarked to Ilie Ceausescu that it was "great to be among friends"; see Funderburk, op. cit., p. 35. Western contacts, together with the manipulation of Romanian nationalist symbols, including Russophobia, also helped Ceausescu's predecessor, Georghiu-Dej, under whose patronage Ceausescu made his career. See Shafir, op. cit., pp. 51–2.

[56] Ibid., p. 177. For Ceausescu's general position, see the discussion in Robert L. Hutchings, *Soviet-East European*

Relations: Consolidation and Conflict; University of Wisconsin Press, Madison, 1987, pp. 41–5. For his speech to the Tenth RCP Congress in 1969, see ibid., p. 121: "By the world socialist system, we understand not a bloc in which the states are fused into a whole, giving up their national sovereignty, but the assertion of socialism as an international force...in several independent states".

[57] See François Fejtö, *A History of the People's Democracies*; Penguin, Harmondsworth, 1974, p. 281. This describes a "resounding speech" by Ceausescu in 1966, which was evidence of "the genuineness of his conversion to the nationalist path".

[58] On Ceausescu's proposition of closer Soviet-Romanian co-operation, see Vladimir Socor, "Romania's Slide into Submission", in Mastny, op. cit., p. 78ff.

[59] See "Exposé on Questions", supra. As late as 1964, Ceausescu was recommending the study of Stalin's *Problems of Leninism* to those wishing to understand Marxism-Leninism as a whole; see Vladimir Tismaneanu, "Ceausescu's Socialism", in *Problems of Communism*, Vol. 34, No. 1, January–February 1985.

[60] Speech in July 1974; quoted in Shafir, op. cit., p. 122.

[61] Quoted in Georgescu, op. cit. Ceausescu was clearly proud of this "insight", since he repeated it when emphasising the need for greater discipline in implementing the party's decisions at a meeting of the Central Committee in November 1985: "Those who do not understand this place themselves on their own outside the...party itself. We are not a discussion club; we are a revolutionary party, struggling for socialism, for communism"; quoted in Tismaneanu, op. cit.

[62] *Frankfurter Allgemeine Zeitung*, 8 July 1988.

[63] Both Pacepa and Funderburk devote a great deal of space to these questions. But Romania's co-operation with US high technology companies, such as Control Data, is now in trouble. Ceausescu told a delegation of US businessmen in May 1988 that whilst Romania "would like to extend this venture [with Control Data] and make it produce more advanced electronics", it was "unfortunately stagnating"; see *Romania Today*, June 1988; and *Lumea*, 13 May 1988.

[64] At first, the Romanian government refused to support the Soviet Union at the UN; and even when Gromyko visited Bucharest in February 1980, it would agree only to call for an end to the "interference of imperialist forces in the internal affairs of other states"; see Hutchings, op. cit., pp. 110–11. By the end of April 1988, however, Ceausescu was congratulating Babrak Karmal on his "revolution"; Shafir, op. cit., pp. 187–90.

[65] See "Exposé on Questions", supra.

[66] Ibid.

[67] *Lumea*, 8 July 1988. Ceausescu receives a steady stream of Israeli visitors too, such as General Ariel Sharon on 18 July 1988.

[68] See Van Tol and Eyal, op. cit. Of course, the bulk of Romanian weaponry comes from the Soviet Union or is based on Soviet designs. As the supply of plundered spare parts reveals, much of its equipment is already out of date. Romania denies that it has "laundered" Norwegian heavy water for Israeli atomic projects; see *Financial Times*, 26 May 1988. Significantly, the chief target of the denials issued by the Romanian press agency, Agerpress, was the Hungarian Party daily, *Nepszabadsag*.

[69] Until 1983, Romania exported around $700 million-worth of weaponry each year. But there has since been a decline in demand. The *SIPRI Yearbook 1987* fails to list any Romanian arms exports, which suggests that Bucharest may have failed to make any figures available. It does, however, refer to Romania's rather ominous capacity to produce chemical weapons, and notes that the percentage of Romanian GDP spent on armaments declined from 2.1 per cent to 1.5 per cent in 1982 – and was estimated at 1.3 per cent for 1986. Romania currently spends only $49 per capita on the military, the lowest proportion in either NATO or the Warsaw Pact. Hungary, by contrast, spends at least $70 per capita.

[70] See Hutchings, op. cit., pp. 111–12.

[71] Georgescu, op. cit. For the Reagan Administration's eagerness to "differentiate" in favour of Romania, see Funderburk, op. cit., *passim*. For Ceausescu's decision to repay the foreign debt of $13 billion in 1981, now down to $5.5 billion, see Crowther, op. cit.

[72] Egypt has become Romania's second largest foreign trade partner after the Soviet Union, although it still does less than 30 per cent as much trade with Romania as the Soviet Union. West Germany is Romania's third most valuable trading partner, ahead of Italy, Iran and the German Democratic Republic. Britain has a trade imba-

lance, importing £92,526,000 in 1987, but exporting only £55,688,000. All such statistics should be treated with caution, however, although commensurate figures are given in the last official *Romania Yearbook*; Bucharest, 1985.

[73] Quoted in Stephen Ashley, "Strains in Soviet-Bulgarian Relations", in Mastny, op. cit., p. 75.

[74] Ceausescu apparently told Richard Nixon in 1982 that Andropov would not succeed Brezhnev; Shafir, op. cit., p. 182.

[75] *Frankfurter Allgemeine Zeitung*, 7 July 1988. On Romania's obstructionism at the CSCE, see *Financial Times*, 28 July 1988. See also Jonathan Luxmoore, *The Helsinki Agreement: Dialogue or Delusion?* Institute for European Defence and Strategic Studies, London, 1986; and George Urban, *Gorbachev: Can the Revolution be Remade?* Institute for European Defence and Strategic Studies, 1988.

[76] Romania has to pay for crude oil imports in convertible currency; see Shafir, op. cit.; and Crowther, op. cit. For Romania's profligacy with fuel, see Paul Gafton, "Economic Malaise and Remedies", in Mastny, op. cit., p. 308. The Slatina aluminium smelting plant alone uses 80 per cent of what ordinary Romanians use at home each year.

[77] See Socor, op. cit.; and Georgescu, op. cit.

[78] For the planned turnover and number of co-operative projects, see Aleksandr Baraulin, "USSR-Romania: Deepening Economic Ties", in *Foreign Trade* (Moscow), May 1988.

[79] In May 1988, the Soviet President, Andrei Gromyko, visited Bucharest to bestow the Order of Lenin on Ceausescu, and to denounce "revanchism" – which probably has less to do with Romanian sentiment about Northern Bukovina and Bessarabia than with Hungarian concern about impending developments in Transylvania; see *Lumea*, 13 May and 20 May 1988. A year earlier, Gorbachev had himself visited Bucharest, where he made some cryptic comments, with reference to *perestroika*: "The concept…is not the expression of anyone's personal will, but the result of the party's collective thought". He also noted "Lenin's thought that 'socialism is not created on orders from above' ". But from Ceausescu's point of view, the most sinister development was Gorbachev's demand that "young people" should be sent to each other's countries to create a "human reservoir for future interaction"; see *Current Digest of the Soviet Press*, Vol. 39, No. 21, 1987. See also Gerhard Wettig, *Soviet Foreign Policy under Gorbachev: New Political Thinking and its Impact*; Institute for European Defence and Strategic Studies, 1988.

[80] For Yugoslav press comment on the refugee question, see *The Independent*, 8 August 1988.

[81] *Financial Times*, 22 June 1988.

[82] *Le Monde*, 24 June 1988.

[83] *Tribuna*, 7 July 1988.

[84] See *Frankfurter Allgemeine Zeitung*, 29 August 1988; and *Financial Times*, 22 June 1988.

[85] Subsequent events seem to indicate that Ceausescu's "willingness to compromise" was only a ruse to enable him to exacerbate the internal contradictions within Hungary. Dissidents were quoted as saying that "the Hungarian regime feels a stronger solidarity with the tyrannical regime of Romania than with the Hungarian minorities". The renewed attack on Budapest later indicated that Grosz did not obtain the concessions from Ceausescu which he claimed. It is doubtful, for instance, that Romania will permit the reunification of families with their defecting members – although Ceausescu might calculate that, if he were to open the gates only temporarily, the flood of refugees would help to destabilise his neighbour and cool Hungarian ardour for the Szeklers' cause; see *The Independent*, 5 September 1988.

[86] See Pacepa, op. cit., pp. 281–2; and *Tribuna Românei*, 1 July 1988.

[87] Hitchings, op. cit., p. 98; and Funderburk, op. cit., *passim*.

[88] Rumours of this kind, often bizarre, are widely prevalent in Romania. For an anthropologist's insights, see Steven Sampson, "Rumours in Socialist Romania", in *Survey*, Vol. 28, No. 4, Winter 1984.

[89] See, for example, Zdenek Mlynar, *Night Frost in Prague: The End of Humane Socialism*; Hurst, London, 1980, pp. 238–9; Sherr, op. cit., pp. 59–61; and Pacepa, op. cit., pp. 214–6 and 409–11.

[90] *Radio Free Europe: Romanian Situation Report*, 3 July 1987, quoting Mihai Botez, who was later beaten up by unidentified attackers. See also ibid., 15 October 1987.

[91] *Le Point*, 30 November 1987. See also Mikhail Gorbachev, *Perestroika: New Thinking for Our Country and the World*; Collins, London, 1978, pp. 162–3; and *Financial Times*, 6 October 1988.

[92] See, for example, *Le Monde*, 3 July 1988.

[93] *Radio Free Europe: Romanian Situation Report*, 13 January 1988. Kiraly is in a good position to know about food exports, not only on account of his previously high rank in the party, but also because, when he wrote the letter, he was still the director of a meat-canning factory at Tirgu-Mures in Transylvania.

[94] Quoted in Funderburk, op. cit., p. 70. Botez made a similar point to Kiraly's, arguing that the export of foodstuffs at a time of acute domestic shortage was "endangering our nation's very biological substance"; *Radio Free Europe: Romanian Situation Report*, 6 March 1987. Apart from the Soviet Union, the Arab countries are the principal importers of Romanian food. Despite the various "food mountains", the EEC countries also import $43 million worth of foodstuffs from Romania, a trivial amount except to the people from whom it is extorted. See Socor, op. cit., p. 82.

[95] *Lumea*, 13 May 1988.

[96] The MPs in question were Jack Aspinall (Cons., Wansdyke), Geraint Howells (Lib., Ceredigon and Pembroke North), James Lamond (Lab., Oldham Central and Royton), David Mudd (Cons., Falmouth and Camborne) and Peter Pike (Lab., Burnley). Several Romanians who spoke to them, at great risk to themselves, were appalled by what they heard in reply.

[97] See Mark Almond, "The Playing Fields of Potsdam", in *Encounter*, August–September 1988.

[98] Apart from the activities in Hungary, strong protests have come from the better organised dissident groups in Poland, Czechoslovakia and the Soviet Union; see *East European Reporter*, Vol. 3, No. 2, March 1988.

[99] *Frankfurter Allgemeine Zeitung*, 8 July 1988.

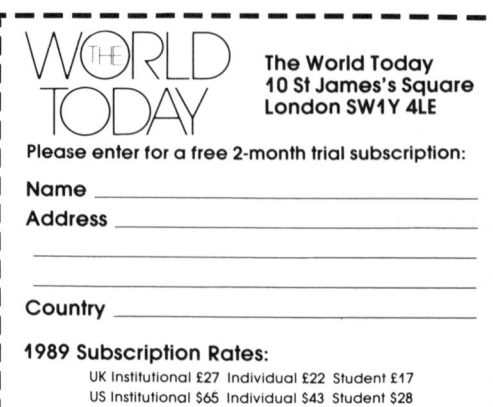

NO END OF A LESSON
Leading articles from
THE TIMES
under Charles Douglas-Home

Foreword by Rupert Murdoch
Introduction by Jessica Douglas-Home

Charles Douglas-Home was Editor of *The Times* from March 1982 until his death in October 1985.

This book, a fitting tribute to a remarkable and courageous journalist, consists of a collection of leaders which appeared during his editorship, mostly on issues relating to defence and international relations, plus a foreword by Rupert Murdoch and an introduction by his widow, the artist Jessica Gwynne.

Defence and international politics were, in fact, subjects which interested and fascinated Charles Douglas-Home throughout his life. Before fulfilling his long-held ambition to edit *The Times*, he had been a lobby correspondent, a defence correspondent, a Foreign Editor, as well as the author of several books on political and defence issues. Although they are written in a commendably simple and direct language, without recourse to technical jargon or the stock phrases which so frequently disfigure writing on inter-state relations and strategic issues, these leaders nevertheless display a considerable knowledge of the subject and many years' reflection. It is possible that the knowledge that his life would be cut short in some sense infused his work with an unusual courage and candour, as well as a compelling sense of urgency to unravel and expose the truth in uncompromising terms.

Despite his confinement to wheelchair and, periodically, to hospital, and despite his frequently stark subject matter, it should not be thought that these pages make gloomy or depressing reading, even when they seek to draw our attention to unpalatable or alarming facts about the international situation. On the contrary, they are full of hope in the moral capacity both of the individual and of free societies to recognise and overcome the dangers and challenges facing them.

"A remarkable book...one that will last forever" – Laurens van der Post
"It is remarkable how well these pieces read...Some of them are models of the leader writer's art" – THE DAILY TELEGRAPH
"Part of the value of such a collection of documents as this is to provide irrefutable dated evidence of what people at a given moment actually thought" – Enoch Powell in THE TIMES

Hardback, 191pp.

Available from the
**Institute for European Defence and Strategic Studies,
13–14 Golden Square, London W1R 3AG
Price £7.50. Postage extra for orders outside UK**

OTHER PUBLICATIONS

PEACE STUDIES: A Critical Survey, by Caroline Cox and Roger Scruton

IDEALISM, REALISM AND THE MYTH OF APPEASEMENT, by Jeane Kirkpatrick

GREECE UNDER PAPANDREOU: Nato's Ambivalent Partner, by John C. Loulis

HEIRS OF CLAUSEWITZ: Change and Continuity in the Soviet War Machine, by C.N. Donnelly

ANTI-AMERICANISM: Steps on a Dangerous Path, by Stephen Haseler

LEGALISED LAWLESSNESS: Soviet Revolutionary Justice, by Richard Pipes

EUROPE'S NEUTRAL STATES: Partners or Profiteers in Western Security? by Stephan Kux

THE HELSINKI AGREEMENT: Dialogue or Delusion? by Jonathan Luxmoore

PRESERVING THE DETERRENT: A Missile Defence for Europe, by Michael Rühle

MALTA ON THE BRINK: From Western Democracy to Libyan Satellite, by Enzo Rossi

LIABILITY OR ASSET? A Policy for the Falkland Islands, by Robert Miller

THE SPETSNAZ THREAT: Can Britain be Defended? by Michael Hickey

THE NEUTRALIST TENDENCY: Defence and the Left in Britain and Germany, by Geoffrey Lee Williams

TERRORIST OR FREEDOM FIGHTER? The Cost of Confusion, by William McGurn

CENTRAL AMERICA: Can Europe Play a Part? by Hugh Thomas

MOSCOW'S AFGHAN WAR: Soviet Motives and Western Interests, by Radek Sikorski

ARMS CONTROL: Has the West Lost its Way? by Robin Brown

NON-OFFENSIVE DEFENCE: A Strategic Contradiction? by David Gates

THE NEW CITY REPUBLICS: Municipal Intervention in Defence, by David Regan

BRITAIN'S SECURITY POLICY: The Modern Soviet View, by Robbin Laird and Susan Clark

THE UN: Assessing Soviet Abuses, by Juliana Geran Pilon and Ralph Kinney Bennett

GORBACHEV: Can the Revolution be Remade? by George Urban

LESS IMPORTANT THAN OPULENCE: The Conservatives and Defence, by Christopher Coker

THE CURE THAT MAY KILL: Unintended Consequences of the INF Treaty, by Angelo Codevilla

MPs AND DEFENCE: A Survey of Parliamentary Knowledge and Opinion, with a commentary by Philip Towle

SOVIET FOREIGN POLICY UNDER GORBACHEV: New Political Thinking and its Impact, by Gerhard Wettig